shreya walia

make it

meatless

100 "Meaty" Recipes that Taste Just Like the Real Thing

Publisher Mike Sanders
Art & Design Director William Thomas
Editorial Director Ann Barton
Senior Editor Olivia Peluso
Assistant Director of Art & Design Becky Batchelor
Photographer Kelley Jordan Schuyler
Food Stylist Lovoni Walker
Photoshoot Chef Ashley Brooks
Recipe Tester Bee Berrie
Copyeditor Christy Wagner
Proofreaders Taylor Plett & Mira S. Park
Indexer Beverlee Day

First American Edition, 2025
Published in the United States by DK Publishing
1745 Broadway, 20th Floor, New York, NY 10019

The authorized representative in the EEA is Dorling Kindersley
Verlag GmbH. Arnulfstr. 124, 80636 Munich, Germany

Copyright © Shreya Walia
DK, a Division of Penguin Random House LLC
25 26 27 28 29   10 9 8 7 6 5 4 3 2 1
001–342937–Aug/2025

All rights reserved.
Without limiting the rights under the copyright reserved above, no part of this publication may be reproduced, stored in or introduced into a retrieval system, or transmitted, in any form, or by any means (electronic, mechanical, photocopying, recording, or otherwise), without the prior written permission of the copyright owner.

No part of this publication may be used or reproduced in any manner for the purpose of training artificial intelligence technologies or systems. In accordance with Article 4(3) of the DSM Directive 2019/790, DK expressly reserves this work from the text and data mining exception.

A catalog record for this book
is available from the Library of Congress.
ISBN 978-0-5938-4780-0

DK books are available at special discounts when purchased in bulk for sales promotions, premiums, fund-raising, or educational use. For details, contact SpecialSales@dk.com

Printed and bound in China

www.dk.com

This book was made with Forest Stewardship Council™ certified paper – one small step in DK's commitment to a sustainable future. Learn more at www.dk.com/uk/information/sustainability

*To my grandma, Lila Wati,
I hope you're enjoying all the bread pakoras
you want in heaven.*

contents

introduction — 6
- why "make it meatless"? — 8
- how to use this book — 10
- the "meats": seitan, plants, mushrooms, and soya — 12
- pantry staples — 14
- equipment — 16

bases, basics & techniques — 19
- chicken 1.0 — 20
- chicken 2.0 — 21
- deli ham — 22
- chicken 3.0 — 24
- classic fried chicken — 27
- beef — 28
- hot dogs — 30
- sausage — 31
- meat crumbles — 33
- italian meatballs — 34
- marinated and battered fish — 36
- bacon — 38
- the best frozen tofu technique — 39

burgers & sandwiches — 41
- gochujang chicken sandwiches — 44
- shroom burger — 47
- buffalo burgers — 48
- buffalo chicken snack wraps — 51
- pulled pork sandwiches — 52
- crispy fish sandwiches with tartar sauce — 55
- pesto caprese sandwiches — 56
- philly cheesesteaks — 59

noods — 61
- chicken pad thai — 64
- pad kee mao — 67
- creamy sun-dried tomato pasta with lemon-caper scallops — 68
- tan tan ramen — 71
- sausage rigatoni — 72
- bucatini carbonara — 75
- chicken chow mein — 76

street food — 79
- korean corn dogs — 82
- carnitas tacos — 85
- chicken fajitas — 86
- chili chicken — 89
- birria tacos — 90
- korean fried chicken bao — 92

soups, curries & stews — 95
- thai chicken red curry — 98
- chicken pho — 101
- gumbo — 102
- italian meatball soup — 105
- chili — 106

snacks & apps — 109
- sesame scallops — 112
- chicken nachos — 115
- chipotle chicken tacos — 116
- chicken taquitos — 119
- ceviche — 120
- enchiladas — 123

takeout 125

- teriyaki chicken 128
- orange chicken 131
- chicken quesadilla........................132
- mongolian beef 135
- chimichangas................................ 136
- chicken fried rice 139
- sofritas 140
- spicy wontons................................ 143
- butter chicken............................... 144
- beef and broccoli 147

fried chicken 149

- chicken nuggets 152
- chicken parmesan 155
- enoki mushroom fried chicken....... 156
- nashville hot chicken tenders 159
- hot honey chicken rolls 160
- chicken and waffles 163
- karaage 164

seared & grilled 167

- steak with garlic-chive butter and asparagus 168
- steak with chimichurri 171
- tandoori chicken rolls 172
- gyros 175

"sea"food 177

- blackened fish 180
- crab cakes 183
- fish tacos 184
- fish and chips................................187
- crab rangoon 188
- fried calamari 191
- parmesan orzo with brown butter scallops 192

pig out 195

- sausage flatbread with truffle pesto 198
- blt 201
- pad kra pao.................................. 202
- sausage and peppers 205
- pork buns 206

not so meaty 209

- mushroom risotto 212
- no-fuss black bean burgers 215
- roasted veggie quesadilla 216
- cajun corn.....................................219
- tofu bahn mi 220
- paneer kathi rolls 223

quickies 225

- buffalo chicken grilled cheese......228
- birria ramen 231
- chili cheese dogs 232
- meatball sliders............................235
- wing platter 236
- barbecue chicken wraps...............239
- bang bang chicken 240

saucy 243

- thai sweet chili sauce 246
- bang bang sauce.......................... 246
- tartar sauce 247
- green chutney.............................. 247
- gochujang sauce 248
- chipotle sauce.............................. 248
- hot honey..................................... 248
- teriyaki sauce 249
- cashew truffle oil pesto 249

- index 250
- acknowledgments........................ 255
- about the author..........................256

introduction

When you grow up in a traditional Indian household, the career options your parents are going to approve of are limited. You have the choice of becoming a doctor, a lawyer, an engineer, or, simply, a family disappointment. Sadly, math gives me a migraine, and the sight of blood makes me queasy. So I was left with the option of becoming a lawyer (or facing certain excommunication). It's not really what I wanted to do, but as far as backup options for careers go, it was pretty illustrious. Well paying. Well respected.

I headed down this carefully chosen path, doing everything I was supposed to do. I graduated from high school, college, and then law school, right on schedule, despite moving all around the world during these formative years. My little family included just me, my dad, and my grandma, and over the years, my dad's job took us from New Delhi, India, to Brampton, Ontario, to London, Ontario, to Dublin, Ireland, to Kalamazoo, Michigan, and then, finally, to Seattle, Washington.

As the years passed and I grew older, I tried every way possible to convince myself that not only was becoming a lawyer the "right" choice, it was something I wanted for myself, too. In many ways, I had learned to love the idea. I enjoyed being on the debate team, participating in Model UN, and taking political science classes. So maybe this was the right career path after all. But it was still hard to silence the nagging thought that perhaps the grass was greener somewhere else—but that I'd never know because I'd be chained to my own front lawn forever.

Just one month before my law school graduation, my grandma passed away. There really aren't enough words in the English language for me to articulate the deep and devastating hole that grief leaves in your heart and mind, and I won't try to. Let's just go with it was bad—really, very, *bad*. Eat six Costco-size danishes in your bed in one sitting type of bad. (True story.)

Just days after my commencement ceremony, my dad and I moved to Los Angeles and I decided to sit for the California bar exam, notorious for its mere 50-ish percent pass rate. There was a lot of crying, grieving, feeling homesick, and experiencing general angst toward life during that time. But the critical part to know is that I passed. Whether it was my family's dream or my own or some strange combination of both, all I knew was that I did it, and I was proud.

Me. A lawyer. It felt so prestigious. So official. I got a thrill every time someone asked me what I did for work, whether they were the barista taking my order at the local coffee shop or a random stranger in the elevator. (Yes, I am, unfortunately, the world's biggest yapper, and I find myself in these situations often.) Having the approval of your family and friends is one thing, but have you seen the twinkle in a complete stranger's eye when you tell them you just passed the bar while you're wearing a ranch-stained Champion hoodie at your dog's day-care facility? (Also true story.) It's unmatched.

But right before I could actually start *practicing* law using the degree I'd worked so hard for, a major global event smacked into the world like a torpedo. You guessed it: Miss Coronavirus arrived, and with a vengeance. Thankfully, the fear and devastation of a life-changing global pandemic was softly counterbalanced by the silly little TikTok videos that millions of us watched from the confines of our homes. We collectively learned how to make banana bread and dalgona (and maybe how to do the occasional dance sequence) while we completely disassociated from what we knew as "normal" life.

I can't remember the exact moment it happened, but one day I decided to start posting content of my own—fun, mostly food-related videos—to pass the time. My morning coffee routine. An easy lunch recipe. Nothing serious, and nothing that seemed worthwhile. But before I knew it, my videos began to gain traction. The first time I broke more than 10,000 views, I ran upstairs to tell my dad. "And next, it'll be a million!" he beamed. And as dads often are, he was right. It didn't happen overnight, but eventually my videos started to perform better and better. People began following me. It blew my mind that anyone, let alone thousands of people, would give me the time of day to drone on about my recipes and that they'd actually care, even in the most miniscule of ways, about my life.

Eventually, I was able to get my first law job and work remotely while the pandemic persisted, but I continued posting online as my new favorite hobby. Before work, after work, even during lunch breaks, I couldn't wait to film—and more importantly, to cook. In fact, I loved it so much, I wondered if I'd finally found my greener grass. I pondered this question for almost three years until April 2023, when I decided to quit my job and pursue my passion. This was a pretty scary choice for a risk-averse girl like me, but it was worth every ounce of fear and self-doubt I had to overcome. Because let me tell you, sometimes your grass has been watered just enough. It's reached its inevitable plateau. Your lawn is pristine and perfectly watered and *sufficient,* but it just can't compare to that vivid stretch of grass across the street you've been staring at your entire life.

why "make it meatless"?

The internet is full of complainers, but one of my points of pride is that no one has ever accused my food of lacking flavor. In fact, I often get comments from viewers who are shocked to learn that the recipes in my videos are totally vegetarian—many people don't even notice until I point it out from time to time. I think this is because vegan and vegetarian food is often pigeonholed as flavorless, bland, and *boring*. So in 2021, I started a little crusade to show people that vegetarian food is just as delicious as its meaty counterparts. Eventually, I turned this into a series, "Make It Meatless," in which I recreated favorite meat dishes using plant-based ingredients. Long story short, that led to the creation of this book.

But despite its popularity, the series wasn't without controversy. A lot of people out there are, dare I say it, *certified meat substitute haters*. This section (and basically this entire book) is also for them. Many folks don't understand why anyone who is vegetarian, vegan, or simply plant-curious would ever want to try a meat substitute if they decided to swear off meat in the first place. Here's my best stab at an explanation.

Why Would Anyone Want to Use a Meat Substitute?

1 **We miss the taste.** Most people who become vegetarian or vegan do so for religious, environmental, or other ethical reasons, not because they don't enjoy the flavor or texture of meat itself. In fact, they may have spent many years consuming meat products and chosen to give them up later in life. It's only natural that they'd miss some of their favorite dishes, especially ones that hold sentimental or cultural significance. Using meat substitutes is a great way for these people to continue enjoying these dishes without compromising their personal beliefs.

2 **It makes the transition to plant-based eating much easier.** Transitions can be difficult. The switch to vegetarianism wasn't very tough for me, but a huge part of that was because I was able to use meat substitutes to satisfy any cravings that did arise. Meat substitutes might not be necessary for everyone or every dish, but they help a lot of people who are struggling with making a big transition in their eating habits. And there's nothing wrong with that.

3 **Why should we be deprived of flavor because of a dietary restriction?** Imagine if we treated other food substitutes with the same disdain some people have for meat substitutes. Sugar-free drinks, gluten-free breads, dairy-free milks and cheeses, non-alcoholic beers ... the list goes on. There's nothing wrong with using substitutes or providing them for people who have different needs, and I see no reason why meat substitutes should be looked down upon. They are a great way to accommodate those with dietary restrictions.

Okay, but If You're a Vegetarian, What's the Point of Making the Substitutes Look Like Meat?

4 **It's not morbid if it's not meat.** Over the years, I've gotten a lot of questions about why I would want to make and eat meat substitutes. People are genuinely confused by the premise that someone would want to make their plants look like meat after they've made the conscious decision to remove meat from their diets for ethical or religious reasons. But what's "morbid" about meat, to a lot of people, is its substance, not its visual aesthetic. As I mentioned earlier, most people who give up meat do so for reasons related to animal abuse, environmental harm, or religious practices, not because they don't like the flavor, taste, or texture of those foods. Making plants look like meat increases visual appeal but doesn't cause any actual harm to animals. No harm, no foul.

5 **You eat with your eyes first.** We have this idiom for a reason. Visual appeal is important to our brains to enhance flavor and curb cravings. It's actually been proven scientifically. A 2014 study noted that the color and texture of a food affects the way people perceive its flavor.[1] So there ya go.

6 **Does actual meat even really look like meat?** Animal products go through an extensive process before they are ready for consumption. Without getting too graphic, any lifelike characteristic of an animal—including feathers, fur, scales, feet, and eyes—is typically removed before it goes onto your grocery store shelves. So when you grab a chicken breast from your local deli, you get a light pink, squishy slab wrapped in cellophane. You know it's chicken. It's labeled as such. But it's much easier to create cognitive dissonance between the package you're holding and the actual living animal it used to be.

Then, before it makes it onto your plate, this chicken breast will be prepped, chopped, seasoned, and cooked. With every added step, it looks less and less like the actual animal it originated from. So when vegetarians and vegans recreate the "meat-like" shapes we're used to seeing in popular dishes, we're essentially just recreating these amorphous shapes we collectively know to be meat but that don't actually have any resemblance to the animals they've come from.

So is it really that strange to put plants through a similar process of transformation, to give them a more appealing appearance? If we can de-feather, batter, season, and fry a real chicken wing, why not go through a similar process with plants, mushrooms, and soya to create a similar look, texture, and flavor?

7 **It's never actually going to taste like meat, so what's the point?** Substitutes are substitutes for a reason. Of course they will never taste 100 percent the same as the real thing. That's okay. The objective here is to get as close as possible to help curb the cravings people might be having for actual meat. This is similar to how regular Coke is better than Diet Coke, but that doesn't mean Diet Coke shouldn't exist.

8 **Okay, but it's so expensive . . .** Yes. There is no denying that creating and even purchasing meat substitutes is expensive. But it's still worth the investment, in my opinion. Spending money on specialty ingredients like vital wheat gluten, textured vegetable protein (TVP), or liquid smoke is no different from splurging on a nice bottle of wine, a fancy cheese, or a high-end cut of meat. The use of such ingredients is not exclusive to plant-based cooking. But for some reason, it seems that vegetarian food gets a disproportionate brunt of the criticism for its costliness. I'm not saying it's fun to spend $17 on a lion's mane mushroom, but I think it's worth the occasional splurge.

---

1 Charles Michel, et al. "A Taste of Kandinsky: Assessing the Influence of the Artistic Visual Presentation of Food on the Dining Experience," *Flavour* 3, no. 7 (2014): https://flavourjournal.biomedcentral.com/articles/10.1186/2044-7248-3-7.

introduction

how to use this book

Rarely does anyone pick up a cookbook and read it cover to cover. That's not how things usually work. You're most likely to go straight to the table of contents like a menu and carefully pick out whatever sounds the most interesting, and rightfully so. Or maybe you're a little more adventurous and start flipping through the pages to see which photos catch your eye before making a decision. Either is totally fine with me! (Hey, I'm just glad you bought the book—thanks, by the way!)

As you're flipping through, here are a few things to keep in mind:

1 **Every recipe in this book is 100 percent meatless.** Although the recipes might be called Classic Fried Chicken (page 27) or Sausage Rigatoni (page 72), please rest assured that no actual chicken or sausage has made its way into the book. What you will find instead are remarkably realistic substitutes. All the recipes in this book are vegetarian, and many are even vegan!

2 **I've provided some base recipes.** The first recipe chapter includes "meat" bases, basics, and important techniques that apply to multiple recipes throughout the book. I created a limited number of core meat substitutes that you'll be able to use not only for recipes in this book, but also as staples in your everyday cooking.

As you become more familiar with the bases, it'll feel easier and easier to make the other recipes that use them. Plus, you can create larger batches of bases at the start of the week and use them to make multiple different recipes throughout the week!

3 **There are QR codes.** Sometimes words just aren't enough. (I know—that's a pretty crazy thing for an author to say.) But certain techniques deserve a visual explanation for clarity. So I've created a set of videos to really explain how to do things right and get the best results possible for these dishes.

10 make it meatless

the "meats":
seitan, plants, mushrooms, and soya

Welcome to the wonderful world of meat substitutes! There are so many ways to make delicious meatless meals, and I've included something for everyone in this book. Here are a few of the meat substitutes you'll find in the recipes:

1 **Seitan.** *Good substitute for chicken, beef, and pork.* Seitan is a meat substitute formulated using wheat gluten. I like to conceptualize seitan in two distinct categories: (1) seitan made using the washed flour method and (2) seitan made using vital wheat gluten. With the washed flour method, you take a large ball of dough and rinse out all the starch via vigorous washing and kneading, leaving behind a thick and stretchy mass of gluten. When cooked (often steamed and/or seared), the gluten forms a remarkable meat-like texture. Vital wheat gluten, on the other hand, has eliminated the need for this laborious process. It is a powdered form of gluten that can be purchased at the grocery store. You simply add water and quickly knead it into a dough that's ready to be cooked. You can further alter the texture of this meat-like dough by mixing in tofu, beans, and plants like jackfruit, which add buoyancy, softness, and additional flavor.

2 **Textured vegetable protein (TVP).** *Good substitute for ground beef and pork.* TVP is a gluten-free meat substitute derived from soy protein. It comes in a dehydrated form and expands almost instantly in hot water, resulting in the perfect meat crumble. It sautés perfectly and is a cheaper alternative to store-bought meatless crumbles.

3 **Tofu.** *Good substitute for chicken.* When prepared and seasoned the right way, tofu can provide a satisfying meat-like texture and flavor. My favorite way to prepare tofu is using the *freezer method* (see The Best Frozen Tofu Technique, page 39), which simply involves freezing unpressed extra-firm tofu, thawing it, and pressing out all the water. Freezing causes the water in the tofu to expand, creating a more porous and somewhat spongy texture that mimics meat. Even though tofu often gets a bad rap for being bland and tasteless, one of its greatest superpowers is its ability to deeply absorb flavors it's soaked in. This makes tofu easily customizable and perfect for use in a variety of recipes.

4 **Banana blossom.** *Good substitute for fish.* Banana blossom is the flower found at the stem of a banana fruit cluster. It has a texture and appearance somewhat similar to artichokes and is very shreddable. Despite its name, banana blossom isn't sweet; it has a mild and savory flavor. You can find canned versions of it at most Asian grocery stores.

5 **Jackfruit.** *Good substitute for pork.* The shreddable texture of jackfruit is perfect for recreating pork dishes. But make sure you purchase *young green jackfruit*; otherwise, you will end up with a dessert instead of a meat substitute.

6 **Oyster mushrooms.** *Good substitute for fried chicken.* The king of mushrooms, oyster mushrooms are what started my obsession with making meatless meals. Even if you're typically a certified mushroom hater, trust me that oyster mushrooms are worth a try. They have a unique, meaty texture, and when battered and fried, they're indistinguishable from chicken wings. These shrooms come in irregular shapes and sizes, but they're easy to mold into various shapes, which works especially well for chicken wings. Fun fact: As fungi, mushrooms are actually closer in composition to animals than plants. Perhaps that has something to do with how meaty their texture is. Who knows? I'm not a food scientist; I'm just a girl.

7 **Enoki mushrooms.** *Good substitute for chicken and fish.* The stringy texture of these mushrooms gives them a unique pull-apart quality that's perfect for emulating chicken. They also naturally have a fishy flavor that can be accentuated to make the perfect faux fish.

8 **King oyster mushrooms.** *Good substitute for pulled pork and seafood.* These mushrooms have a dense texture and uniform shape, which makes them easy to turn into scallops or calamari. Plus, they can be easily shredded using a fork to mimic pulled meats like pork or even beef.

9 **Lion's mane mushrooms.** *Good substitute for beef or chicken.* These might look a little like fuzzy cauliflower, but the fibrous texture inside lion's mane mushrooms is meaty. I think they work best for beef or chicken dishes, but they could also be pulled apart or marinated to resemble pork.

introduction

pantry staples

This is the stuff I recommend you have in your pantry to make your food taste good. These oils, vinegars, spices, and sauces add richness and depth of flavor, while the flours and canned goods help create the meat-like textures you're craving.

oils and vinegars
- Canola oil
- Chili oil
- Olive oil
- Sesame oil
- Distilled white vinegar
- Mirin
- Rice vinegar

sweet stuff
- Brown sugar
- Honey
- Maple syrup

spicy sauces
- Chili crisp
- Gochujang paste
- Harissa paste
- Sambal oelek
- Sriracha

ingredients for depth and umami
- Dark soy sauce
- Kombu seaweed
- Light soy sauce
- Liquid smoke
- Nutritional yeast
- Red miso paste
- Vegetable bouillon paste
- Wakame seaweed
- White miso paste

dry spices
- Arbol chiles
- Bay leaves
- Black cardamom
- Black pepper
- Cayenne
- Chili powder
- Coriander
- Cumin
- Flaky sea salt
- Garam masala
- Garlic powder
- Gochugaru flakes
- Green cardamom
- Himalayan salt
- Kashmiri red chile powder
- Kasoori methi (fenugreek leaves)
- Mango powder
- Onion powder
- Oregano
- Red pepper flakes
- Sea salt
- Smoked paprika
- Thyme
- Turmeric
- White pepper

spice blends
- Cajun seasoning
- Italian seasoning
- Old Bay Seasoning

ingredients for color
- Beetroot powder
- Red gel food coloring

flours
- All-purpose flour
- Baking powder
- Baking soda
- Cornstarch
- Panko breadcrumbs
- Sweet potato flour
- Tapioca flour
- Tapioca starch
- Textured vegetable protein (TVP)
- Vital wheat gluten

canned and bottled ingredients
- Chickpeas
- Tomato paste
- White navy beans
- Vegetable broth

make it meatless

equipment

First things first: I don't think you *need* any fancy tools or equipment to cook delicious food. But for those of you who are curious about the staple items I used in my own kitchen while creating these recipes, here they are:

- Air fryer
- Baking sheet
- Bench scraper (for cutting dough and seitan)
- Box grater
- Cooking chopsticks
- Cutting board
- Deep baking dish (9 × 13 inches)
- Dry and wet measuring cups and spoons
- Grating plate (for ginger and garlic)
- Jar spatula (for scraping the sides of your blender)
- Knives
- Lemon squeezer

- Manual food chopper (like Slap Chop)
- Mincer
- Mixing bowls
- Pots (small, medium, and large)
- Scale
- Sieve
- Skillets (small, medium, and large)
- Small blender
- Spatula
- Steamer basket setup (metal and bamboo)
- Stirring spoons
- Tongs
- Whisk

bases
basics
techn

> Let's start with the basics. Here's everything you need to know to kick-start your meatless journey.

chicken 1.0

makes about 12 ounces

Chicken 1.0 is the perfect quick and dirty introduction to seitan that you can make in a pinch! It includes minimal ingredients and comes together quickly without sacrificing flavor. This lightly seasoned seitan "chicken" makes a perfect base for any dish when you're too tired to pull out the big guns (aka a steamer basket you'll have to wash later). Use this recipe as a substitute for Chicken 2.0 (page 21) or Chicken 3.0 (page 24) when you're running low on time (or patience), or if you're looking for a seitan texture that is softer and chewier.

- 1 cup water
- 2 teaspoons vegetable bouillon paste
- 1 cup vital wheat gluten (I recommend Anthony's)
- 2 tablespoons rice flour
- 2 tablespoons tapioca flour
- 1 teaspoon salt
- ½ teaspoon garlic powder
- ½ teaspoon onion powder
- ¼ cup neutral oil (such as canola or vegetable)

1. Add the water and bouillon paste to a large bowl, and mix until the bouillon paste is dissolved. Add the vital wheat gluten, rice flour, tapioca flour, salt, garlic powder, and onion powder. Mix well and knead in the bowl until a soft dough forms, about 5 minutes. The dough will be wet and spongy. Gently squeeze out the excess water.

2. Pull apart the dough to form about 14 small chicken strips. Firmly squeeze and shape the dough to your preference.

3. Heat the oil in a medium skillet over medium heat. Add the chicken pieces, and fry until crispy and golden brown, 3 to 5 minutes (see Note). Remove the chicken from the skillet, and serve immediately.

note

If you prefer a less-chewy texture, add ¼ cup water to the skillet and cover it with a lid to gently steam your seitan after it's crisped in step 3. Heat until the water is fully evaporated, 3 to 5 minutes.

20   **make it meatless**

chicken 2.0

makes about 2 pounds

Seitan can be customized in many ways to resemble different meats. You can combine it with tofu, beans, or a variety of starches, for example, to bring out certain meaty flavors. For chicken, I've found that adding navy beans and white miso paste best mimics the mild, savory flavor of chicken. This chicken is easy to tear apart into bite-size pieces and perfect for eating right away or sautéing to a light crisp.

- 1 cup canned navy beans, drained but not rinsed
- 1 tablespoon white miso paste
- 2 teaspoons vegetable bouillon paste
- ½ teaspoon garlic powder
- ½ teaspoon onion powder
- 1 teaspoon salt
- 2 cups water
- 2¼ cups vital wheat gluten (I recommend Anthony's)

1. Place the beans, miso paste, bouillon paste, garlic powder, onion powder, salt, and water in a small blender, and blend until smooth. Transfer to a large bowl, scraping the sides of the blender to ensure all the mixture is removed.

2. Add the vital wheat gluten, and mix to combine.

3. Knead the dough until it is soft and springy, 7 to 10 minutes. Split the dough into two balls, and wrap each ball in foil.

4. Set up a steamer basket: Place a metal steamer basket in a large pot. The steamer basket should be small enough to fit inside the pot with the lid closed. Add enough water to the pot to reach just below the steamer basket. (The basket should not be submerged in the water.) Bring the water to a boil over high heat and then reduce the heat to medium.

5. Add the dough, cover, and steam until the dough firms up, about 1 hour. Make sure to top up the pot with water as needed. There should always be at least 1 inch of water in the bottom of the pot.

6. Use tongs to remove the dough from the steamer basket. Let the dough cool in the foil at room temperature for about 1 hour before using.

7. Serve the chicken by tearing it into pieces, slicing it, or using it however you like. Or store in the refrigerator for up to 5 days. To store, unwrap the chicken from the foil, wrap tightly in plastic wrap, and place in an airtight container or zipper bag. To reheat, unwrap the chicken, cover it with a damp paper towel, and microwave it until tender and warmed through the center. (Reheating time will vary depending on the quantity of chicken and the size of the pieces.)

watch me make this!

bases, basics & techniques

deli ham

serves 6

Ice Spice is gonna be mad if you're not shaking your ass to this recipe. This seitan deli ham is perfect to keep in your fridge for weekly meal prep. Simply slice it and use it to add a hammy touch to your sandwiches and wraps.

8 ounces extra-firm tofu
2 teaspoons soy sauce
1 teaspoon vegetable bouillon paste
1 teaspoon ponzu sauce
¼ teaspoon garlic powder
¼ teaspoon onion powder
5 drops red gel food coloring
1 cup vital wheat gluten (I recommend Anthony's)

1. Place the tofu, soy sauce, bouillon paste, ponzu sauce, garlic powder, onion powder, and food coloring in a blender, and blend to form a smooth, pudding-like consistency. Transfer to a large bowl, scraping the sides of the blender to ensure all the mixture is removed.

2. Add the vital wheat gluten, and mix well. Turn out the mixture onto a flat surface, and knead to form a slightly tough and springy dough, about 5 minutes.

3. Form the dough into a ball and then wrap it tightly in foil, using the foil to help the ball hold its shape.

4. Set up a steamer basket: Place a metal steamer basket in a large pot. The steamer basket should be small enough to fit inside the pot with the lid closed. Add enough water to the pot to reach just below the steamer basket. (The basket should not be submerged in the water.) Bring the water to a boil over high heat and then reduce the heat to medium.

5. Add the dough, cover, and steam until the dough firms up, about 30 minutes. Make sure to top up the water in the pot as needed. There should always be at least 1 inch of water in the bottom of the pot.

6. Use tongs to remove the dough from the steamer basket. Let the dough cool in the foil at room temperature for about 20 minutes before unwrapping.

7. Slice and serve. Or store whole in the refrigerator for up to 5 days. To store, unwrap the dough from the foil, wrap tightly in plastic wrap, and place in an airtight container or zipper bag.

make it meatless

chicken 3.0

makes about 1 pound

Seitan has the tendency to dry out when it's overcooked. But have no fear: Chicken 3.0 is here! The combination of tofu and tapioca starch in this recipe keeps the seitan chicken buoyant and tender whether you're deep-frying, shallow-frying, or sautéing.

8 ounces extra-firm tofu
2 tablespoons olive oil
1 tablespoon white miso paste
2 teaspoons vegetable bouillon paste
1 teaspoon garlic powder
1 teaspoon onion powder
1 teaspoon salt
1 cup vital wheat gluten (I recommend Anthony's)
1 tablespoon tapioca starch

1. Place the tofu, olive oil, miso paste, bouillon paste, garlic powder, onion powder, and salt in a blender, and blend to form a thick mixture the consistency of hummus. Transfer to a medium bowl, scraping the sides of the blender to ensure all the mixture is removed.

2. Add the vital wheat gluten and tapioca starch, and mix to combine.

3. Turn the mixture onto a flat surface, and knead to form a spongy dough, about 5 minutes. Wrap the dough in foil.

4. Set up a steamer basket: Place a metal steamer basket in a large pot. The steamer basket should be small enough to fit inside the pot with the lid closed. Add enough water to the pot to reach just below the steamer basket. (The basket should not be submerged in the water.) Bring the water to a boil over high heat and then reduce the heat to medium.

5. Add the dough, cover, and steam until the dough firms up, about 1 hour and 15 minutes. Make sure to top up the pot with water as needed. There should always be at least 1 inch of water in the bottom of the pot.

6. Use tongs to remove the dough from the steamer basket. Let the dough cool in the foil at room temperature for 30 minutes before using.

7. Serve the chicken by tearing it into pieces, slicing it, or using it however you like. Or store in the refrigerator for up to 5 days. To store, unwrap the chicken from the foil, wrap tightly in plastic wrap, and place in an airtight container or zipper bag. To reheat, unwrap the chicken, cover it with a damp paper towel, and microwave it until tender and warmed through the center. (Reheating time will vary depending on the quantity of chicken and the size of the pieces.)

watch me make this!

24 **make it meatless**

classic fried chicken

serves 2

Fun fact: This is the recipe that inspired this entire book. If there's only one recipe you make from *Make It Meatless*, it should be this one. This recipe was my introduction to oyster mushrooms, and it convinced me that mushrooms can, in fact, taste like chicken if prepared the right way. Plus, you can pretty much fry anything in this delicious batter and it'll taste good.

1. Create a batter station. **Make the dry batter:** Whisk together the flour, breadcrumbs, chile powder, garlic powder, onion powder, salt, cumin, and white pepper in a medium bowl.

2. **Make the wet batter:** Whisk together the flour, salt, chile powder, garlic powder, onion powder, cumin, white pepper, and water in a separate medium bowl.

3. Break the oyster mushrooms into large pieces.

4. Dip each mushroom piece into the wet batter and then the dry batter, making sure it's evenly coated each time. Set aside the battered pieces on a plate.

5. Heat enough oil in a medium pot over medium heat to completely cover the mushrooms. To check if the oil is ready, add a few drops of the wet batter to the oil. The batter should start gently sizzling. If the oil starts sputtering, it is too hot.

6. Add the mushrooms to the pot, and fry until they are golden brown and crispy, about 5 minutes.

7. Transfer the mushrooms to a paper towel to soak up the excess oil before serving.

8. Squeeze lemon juice (if using) generously on top, and serve.

dry batter
- 1 cup all-purpose flour
- 1 cup Japanese-style panko breadcrumbs
- 1 teaspoon Kashmiri red chile powder
- 1 teaspoon garlic powder
- 1 teaspoon onion powder
- 1 teaspoon salt
- ¼ teaspoon ground cumin
- ¼ teaspoon white pepper

wet batter
- 1 cup all-purpose flour
- 1 teaspoon salt
- 1 teaspoon Kashmiri red chile powder
- 1 teaspoon garlic powder
- 1 teaspoon onion powder
- ¼ teaspoon ground cumin
- ¼ teaspoon white pepper
- 1¼ cups water

- 2 large oyster mushrooms (about 8 ounces)
- Vegetable oil, for frying
- Lemon juice, for serving, optional

watch me make this!

bases, basics & techniques

beef

makes about 18 ounces

Slice this beef for Philly Cheesesteaks (page 59) or sauté it for a quick Beef and Broccoli stir-fry (page 147)! The combination of dark soy sauce, nutritional yeast, and beetroot powder adds umami and earthiness to flavor this seitan beef recipe.

One 15.5-ounce can navy beans, drained but not rinsed
¼ cup water
2 tablespoons dark soy sauce
1 tablespoon nutritional yeast
2 teaspoons beetroot powder
2 teaspoons vegetable bouillon paste
2 teaspoons tomato paste
1 teaspoon garlic powder
1 teaspoon onion powder
1 teaspoon salt
1¾ cups vital wheat gluten (I recommend Anthony's)

1. Place the beans, water, soy sauce, nutritional yeast, beetroot powder, bouillon paste, tomato paste, garlic powder, onion powder, and salt in a blender, and blend to form a smooth puree.

2. Place the vital wheat gluten in a large bowl. Pour the puree on top. Use a small spatula to scrape the sides of the blender to remove all the puree. Use the spatula to gently mix the dough together before switching to using your hands.

3. Turn the dough onto a flat surface, and firmly knead with your hands for about 5 minutes, making sure to pull the dough apart and press it back together to create texture.

4. Divide the dough into two balls, and wrap them in foil.

5. Set up a steamer basket: Place a metal steamer basket in a large pot. The steamer basket should be small enough to fit inside the pot with the lid closed. Add enough water to the pot to reach just below the steamer basket. (The basket should not be submerged in the water.) Bring the water to a boil over high heat and then reduce the heat to medium.

6. Add the dough, cover, and steam until the dough firms up, about 45 minutes. Make sure to top up the water in the pot as needed. There should always be at least 1 inch of water in the bottom of the pot.

7. Use tongs to remove the dough from the steamer basket. Let the dough cool in the foil at room temperature for about 20 minutes before using.

8. Serve the beef by tearing it into pieces, slicing it, or using it however you like. Or store in the refrigerator for up to 5 days. To store, unwrap the beef from the foil, wrap tightly in plastic wrap, and place in an airtight container or zipper bag. To reheat, unwrap the beef, cover it with a damp paper towel, and microwave it until tender and warmed through the center. (Reheating time will vary depending on the quantity of beef and the size of the pieces.)

watch me make this!

make it meatless

hot dogs

makes 4 hot dogs

I'll skip the tawdry wiener jokes and let you fill in the blanks. These classic hot dogs are made with a tofu and vital wheat gluten base to create the perfect bouncy texture you're looking for in a hot dog. Serve on a bun with ketchup, yellow mustard, and lots of relish. Or use them to make Korean Corn Dogs (page 82) or Chili Cheese Dogs (page 232).

8 ounces extra-firm tofu
3 tablespoons water
1 tablespoon ketchup
2 teaspoons vegetable bouillon paste
2 teaspoons soy sauce
½ teaspoon garlic powder
½ teaspoon onion powder
½ teaspoon salt
¼ teaspoon smoked paprika
3 to 5 drops red gel food coloring
1 cup vital wheat gluten (I recommend Anthony's)
¼ cup tapioca starch
5 tablespoons olive oil, divided

1. Place the tofu, water, ketchup, bouillon paste, soy sauce, garlic powder, onion powder, salt, paprika, and food coloring in a blender, and blend until smooth. Transfer to a large bowl, scraping the sides of the blender to ensure all the mixture is removed.

2. Add the vital wheat gluten and tapioca starch, and mix well. Turn out the dough onto a flat surface, and knead until smooth, 5 minutes. The dough should be a dark pinkish red.

3. Divide the dough into four pieces, and roll out each piece into a hot dog shape using your palms. Rub each hot dog with 1 tablespoon of olive oil; make sure it is evenly coated.

4. Tightly wrap each hot dog in foil, twisting the ends closed to help form the shape.

5. Set up a steamer basket: Place a metal steamer basket in a large pot. The steamer basket should be small enough to fit inside the pot with the lid closed. Add enough water to the pot to reach just below the steamer basket. (The basket should not be submerged in the water.) Bring the water to a boil over high heat and then reduce the heat to medium.

6. Add the hot dogs, cover, and steam until the hot dogs firm up, about 30 minutes. Make sure to top up the water in the pot as needed. There should always be at least 1 inch of water in the bottom of the pot.

7. Use tongs to remove the hot dogs from the steamer basket. Let them cool in the foil at room temperature for 1 hour before unwrapping.

8. Heat a medium skillet over medium heat. Add the remaining 1 tablespoon of olive oil and the hot dogs, and cook until gently browned, 2 to 3 minutes. Serve.

sausage

makes 4 sausages

This sausage is made to be truly versatile. You can crumble it and add it to pastas and soups or on top of flatbread, or you can slice it and toss some in your weeknight one-pot dinner. I've suggested Italian seasoning here for the flavor, but you can substitute your favorite seasonings to create a variety of custom sausage recipes. Try Cajun seasoning, lemon pepper, lots of red pepper flakes, or whatever else you like to get the flavor profiles you desire.

8 ounces extra-firm tofu
2 tablespoons tomato paste
1 tablespoon soy sauce
2 teaspoons Italian seasoning, optional
2 teaspoons vegetable bouillon paste
1 teaspoon red pepper flakes
½ teaspoon salt
Black pepper, to taste
4 drops red gel food coloring
¾ cup vital wheat gluten (I recommend Anthony's)
⅓ cup finely chopped yellow onion, optional
3 tablespoons tapioca starch
2 teaspoons minced garlic
3 tablespoons olive oil

1. Add the tofu, tomato paste, soy sauce, Italian seasoning, if using, bouillon paste, red pepper flakes, salt, pepper, and food coloring to a blender, and blend to form a paste. Transfer to a large bowl, scraping the sides of the blender to ensure all the mixture is removed.

2. Add the vital wheat gluten, onion, if using, tapioca starch, and garlic, and mix well with a spatula. Turn out the dough onto a flat surface, and knead until it is springy and firm, making sure to pull and stretch the dough as much as possible to create texture, about 5 minutes.

3. Divide the dough into four pieces, and roll each into a sausage shape using your palms. Tightly wrap each sausage in foil, twisting the ends closed to help form the shape.

4. Set up a steamer basket: Place a metal steamer basket in a large pot. The steamer basket should be small enough to fit inside the pot with the lid closed. Add enough water to the pot to reach just below the steamer basket. (The basket should not be submerged in the water.) Bring the water to a boil over high heat and then reduce the heat to medium.

5. Add the sausages, cover, and steam until the sausages are firm, about 40 minutes. Make sure to top up the water in the pot as needed. There should always be at least 1 inch of water at the bottom of the pot.

6. Use tongs to remove the sausages from the steamer basket. Let them cool in the foil at room temperature for 20 minutes before unwrapping. Cook or store in an airtight container in the refrigerator for up to 5 days.

7. To cook, unwrap the foil, and slice the sausages into ½-inch-thick pieces. Heat the olive oil in a large skillet over medium heat, add the sausages, and cook until slightly charred, 2 to 3 minutes on each side. Serve.

sausage crumbles

To make sausage crumbles, break apart the sausages in step 7 (instead of cutting them) by placing them on a cutting board and pressing down firmly using the palm of your hand. Heat the olive oil as directed, add the crumbles, and cook for 2 to 3 minutes.

watch me make this!

bases, basics & techniques

meat crumbles

makes about 2 cups

I would never make you pay $15 for a tiny bag of meatless meat crumbles from your local Whole Foods. Make these quick and easy meaty crumbles using textured vegetable protein (TVP) instead!

1. Place the hot water, vegetable bouillon paste, soy sauce, garlic powder, onion powder, tomato paste, salt, and pepper in a medium bowl, and mix to combine.

2. Add the TVP, and mix well. Let the mixture sit until the TVP has absorbed the water and doubled in size, about 5 minutes.

3. Using a spoon, evenly sprinkle the vital wheat gluten over the TVP mixture. Gently toss the mixture together with your hands until the vital wheat gluten is evenly incorporated.

4. Cook or store in a zipper bag in the refrigerator for up to 5 days.

5. To cook, heat ½ to 1 tablespoon of olive oil in a medium skillet over medium heat. Add ¼ cup of the meat crumbles at a time (to ensure even cooking), and sauté until they crisp up and take on a deep brown color, about 5 minutes. Repeat with the remaining crumbles, and serve.

---

1 cup hot water
2 teaspoons vegetable bouillon paste
1½ teaspoons dark soy sauce
1 teaspoon garlic powder
1 teaspoon onion powder
1 teaspoon tomato paste
½ teaspoon salt
Black pepper, to taste
1¼ cups textured vegetable protein (TVP)
6 tablespoons vital wheat gluten (I recommend Anthony's)
Olive oil, for sautéing

watch me make this!

bases, basics & techniques   33

italian meatballs

makes 8 meatballs

There's something magical about a simple meatball and spaghetti dinner that I just couldn't live without after I went vegetarian. Here, we're using two of our favorite powerhouse ingredients—vital wheat gluten and textured vegetable protein (TVP)—to perfectly mimic the texture of meatballs. Add these meatballs to pastas or soups or make a meatball sub for a satisfying meatless meal!

- 1 cup hot water
- 2 teaspoons vegetable bouillon paste
- 1 tablespoon tomato paste
- ½ cup textured vegetable protein (TVP)
- 1½ cups vital wheat gluten (I recommend Anthony's)
- 1 tablespoon finely chopped fresh parsley
- 2 teaspoons Italian seasoning
- 1 teaspoon salt
- 1 teaspoon garlic powder
- 1 teaspoon onion powder
- Black pepper, to taste

1. Pour the hot water into a large bowl. Add the bouillon paste and tomato paste, and stir until dissolved.

2. Add the TVP, mix to combine, and let the mixture rest for 5 minutes.

3. Add the vital wheat gluten, parsley, Italian seasoning, salt, garlic powder, onion powder, and pepper, and use your hands to mix the ingredients until evenly combined. Add a splash of water, if needed, to help the mixture hold together.

4. Divide the mixture into eight equal portions (about 2 ounces each), and shape each into a meatball. (Some of the TVP might fall out of the mixture and not stick entirely. That's okay. This creates little air pockets throughout the meatball, which add texture.) Wrap each meatball in foil.

5. Set up a steamer basket: Place a metal steamer basket in a large pot. The steamer basket should be small enough to fit inside the pot with the lid closed. Add enough water to the pot to reach just below the steamer basket. (The basket should not be submerged in the water.) Bring the water to a boil over high heat and then reduce the heat to medium.

6. Add the meatballs, cover, and steam until the meatballs are firm, about 40 minutes. Make sure to top up the water in the pot as needed. There should always be at least 1 inch of water in the bottom of the pot.

7. Use tongs to remove the meatballs from the pot. Let cool for 20 minutes before unwrapping and serving. Or store in an airtight container in the refrigerator for up to 5 days.

34 **make it meatless**

marinated and battered fish

serves 2 to 4

This delicious, fishy marinade and light, airy frying batter are perfect for transforming plant-based ingredients into the meatless seafood of your dreams. This marinade and batter work particularly well with banana blossoms, but they would also work well with jackfruit or mushrooms of your choice!

1 **Make the marinade:** Combine the soy sauce, olive oil, lemon juice, chile powder, garlic powder, onion powder, paprika, salt, and pepper in a large bowl.

2 **Make the fishy flavor (if using):** Pour the hot water into a small bowl. Add the kombu and dried seaweed, and soak for 20 minutes. Add 2 or 3 tablespoons of the liquid to the marinade, and mix well.

3 **Make the fish:** Massage the marinade into the banana blossoms until evenly distributed and then submerge the blossoms in the marinade and set in the refrigerator to marinate for 1 hour.

4 **Make the batter:** Whisk together the flour, cornstarch, Old Bay, baking soda, and salt in a medium bowl. Add ½ cup of seltzer, and mix until well combined. If you need to loosen the batter, add up to ¼ cup more seltzer, 1 tablespoon at a time, mixing well after each addition. (The consistency should look similar to pancake batter.) Add 1 or 2 tablespoons of the fishy flavor to the batter, if using, and mix well.

5 Remove the banana blossoms from the refrigerator, and evenly coat them in the batter, letting the excess drip off.

6 Heat 2 inches of canola oil in a medium skillet over medium heat. Add the banana blossoms, and fry until crispy and golden brown, about 5 minutes. Serve.

fishy marinade
- 3 tablespoons soy sauce
- 2 tablespoons olive oil
- 1 tablespoon lemon juice
- 1 teaspoon Kashmiri red chile powder
- ½ teaspoon garlic powder
- ½ teaspoon onion powder
- ¼ teaspoon smoked paprika
- Salt and black pepper, to taste

fishy flavor, optional
- ½ cup hot water
- 2 pieces kombu
- Small handful dried wakame seaweed (about 2 tablespoons)

fish
- One 18-ounce can banana blossoms (9 ounces drained)
- Canola oil, for frying

fishy batter
- ½ cup all-purpose flour
- 3 tablespoons cornstarch
- 1 teaspoon Old Bay Seasoning
- 1 teaspoon baking soda
- ½ teaspoon salt
- ½ to ¾ cup unflavored seltzer

watch me make this!

make it meatless

bacon

serves 2

This is a quick and easy shroomy bacon recipe. Add it to a BLT (page 201), enjoy it with some eggs and hash browns, or chop and crumble it over a loaded baked potato.

1 tablespoon dark soy sauce
2 teaspoons olive oil
½ teaspoon liquid smoke
¼ teaspoon garlic powder
¼ teaspoon onion powder
⅛ teaspoon apple cider vinegar
⅛ teaspoon smoked paprika
3½ ounces oyster mushrooms

1. Preheat an air fryer to 400°F.
2. Combine the soy sauce, olive oil, liquid smoke, garlic powder, onion powder, apple cider vinegar, and paprika in a small bowl.
3. Add the mushrooms, and massage them well with the marinade. Let sit for 10 minutes.
4. Squeeze out the excess marinade from the mushrooms using your hands.
5. Wrap the mushrooms in a paper towel, and squeeze gently one more time to remove the excess liquid.
6. Place the mushrooms in the air fryer for 5 minutes, until the edges are nice and crispy.
7. Break apart into your desired size before serving.

bacon bits

To make bacon bits, chop the cooked bacon into small pieces and return them to the air fryer for 2 minutes for an added crisp.

make it meatless

the best frozen tofu technique

serves 2

Before I explain the best way to freeze tofu, I gotta explain the original technique. Most store-bought tofu is packaged in water to keep the tofu moist and preserve its texture. Tofu is porous, so it absorbs this water. But when it's frozen, the water inside expands and further enhances the tofu's porous texture, making it even more meat-like! In the original frozen tofu technique, the tofu is thawed, pressed, and prepared. If you want to stop right there, you absolutely can. But I figured, why not add some extra layers of flavor to this technique? So before freezing, we're going to turn our tofu water into a rich marinade instead.

One 15.5-ounce block extra-firm tofu
1 tablespoon soy sauce
2 teaspoons vegetable bouillon paste
2 teaspoons white miso paste
1 teaspoon nutritional yeast
½ teaspoon garlic powder
½ teaspoon onion powder

1 Remove the tofu from the packaging and set aside on a plate.

2 Drain the water from the tofu container into a large zipper bag. Add the soy sauce, bouillon paste, miso paste, nutritional yeast, garlic powder, and onion powder. Use your finger to press and squeeze the bag until the miso and bouillon pastes dissolve.

3 Add the tofu to the bag, and let it soak at room temperature for 15 minutes.

4 Place the bag in the freezer, and freeze overnight.

5 Before using, thaw the tofu in the refrigerator overnight. Remove it from the bag, wrap it in a few sheets of paper towel, and press for 15 minutes under a heavy pan to remove the excess moisture. Then use in your favorite recipe.

bases, basics & techniques

burge
sandw

Burgers and sandos
and wraps—oh my!

gochujang chicken sandwiches

serves 2

Sugar, spice, and everything nice–this crispy gochujang chicken sandwich is what dreams are made of. It's the perfect balance of savory, sweet, and spicy, with the right touch of tartness, that will keep you coming back for more.

1 **Make the chicken:** For the best flavor, prepare the tofu using The Best Frozen Tofu Technique (page 39). Otherwise, drain the tofu, wrap it in paper towels, and press it under a heavy pot or pan for 15 minutes to remove the excess water.

2 Cut the tofu horizontally into two slabs. I like to cut each slab into a long oval shape, resembling a chicken breast, by cutting off the corners.

3 Create a batter station. **Make the wet batter:** Whisk together the flour, garlic powder, gochugaru, onion powder, salt, and water in a medium shallow bowl until no lumps remain. **Make the dry batter:** Mix together the flour, panko breadcrumbs, garlic powder, gochugaru, onion powder, and salt in a separate medium shallow bowl.

4 Evenly coat each slab of tofu in the wet batter, let the excess drip off, and then gently place the tofu into the dry batter and coat evenly on both sides. Gently press the dry batter into the tofu so it adheres well.

5 Heat about 2 inches of oil in a heavy medium skillet over medium heat. Gently place the tofu slabs, one at a time, into the skillet, and cook until crispy and golden brown, about 5 minutes. Remove the tofu from the skillet and let cool on a paper towel–lined plate.

6 **Make the gochujang sauce:** Mix the gochujang, soy sauce, rice vinegar, sesame oil, and honey in a small bowl.

7 **Make the kimchi slaw:** Combine the kimchi, mayonnaise, soy sauce, and sesame oil in a small bowl.

8 Use a basting brush to coat the tofu with the gochujang sauce.

9 To assemble the sandwiches, divide the chicken and kimchi slaw between the buns. Evenly divide the lettuce, tomato slices, mayonnaise, and dill pickles, and layer on each sandwich. Serve.

chicken
- One 16-ounce block extra-firm tofu
- Canola oil, for frying

wet batter
- ½ cup all-purpose flour
- ½ teaspoon garlic powder
- ½ teaspoon gochugaru flakes
- ½ teaspoon onion powder
- ½ teaspoon salt
- 1¼ cup water

dry batter
- ½ cup all-purpose flour
- ½ cup Japanese-style panko breadcrumbs
- ½ teaspoon garlic powder
- ½ teaspoon gochugaru flakes
- ½ teaspoon onion powder
- ½ teaspoon salt

gochujang sauce
- ¼ cup gochujang paste
- 2 teaspoons soy sauce
- 1 teaspoon rice vinegar
- 1 teaspoon toasted sesame oil
- 1 tablespoon plus 1 teaspoon honey

kimchi slaw
- ¼ cup vegan kimchi, finely chopped
- 3 tablespoons mayonnaise
- 2 teaspoons soy sauce
- ¼ teaspoon toasted sesame oil

for serving
- 2 brioche buns, toasted
- Iceberg lettuce
- Tomato slices
- Kewpie mayonnaise
- Sandwich dill pickle chips

make it meatless

shroom burger

serves 1

I'm not going to say this mozzarella-stuffed mushroom burger is a dead ringer for a certain fast-food chain's burger, but I'm also not *not* going to say that . . .

1. Preheat an air fryer to 400°F.

2. Remove the stems from the mushrooms. With a small spoon, scrape around the underside of the mushroom caps to remove the gills.

3. Brush each mushroom with 1 teaspoon of olive oil, and fry in the air fryer for 8 to 10 minutes. The mushrooms should still look juicy. Remove from the air fryer and let cool at room temperature for 5 minutes.

4. Wrap the mushrooms in paper towels, and gently squeeze to remove any excess moisture.

5. Break the mozzarella slices into pieces, and press them between the two mushrooms so the cheese becomes the filling. Wrap the mushrooms in paper towels, and gently squeeze again to remove any remaining excess moisture.

6. Create a batter station. **Make the wet batter:** Combine the flour, chile powder, garlic powder, onion powder, salt, cayenne, cumin, paprika, pepper, and water in a medium bowl.

7. **Make the dry batter:** Combine the flour, panko breadcrumbs, chile powder, garlic powder, onion powder, salt, cayenne, cumin, paprika, and pepper in a separate medium bowl.

8. Coat the mushroom patty in the wet batter and then in the dry batter.

9. Heat about 1 inch of canola oil in a medium skillet over medium heat. Add the mushroom patty, and fry until crispy and golden brown, 3 to 4 minutes per side.

10. **Make the harissa lime aioli:** Combine the mayonnaise, harissa, and lime juice in a small bowl.

11. Spread the aioli on the burger bun, and add the burger patty. Top with romaine lettuce, tomatoes, red onions, pickles, and any other toppings you like, and serve.

2 portobello mushrooms
2 teaspoons olive oil
2 to 3 slices low-moisture, part-skim mozzarella
Canola oil, for frying

wet batter
½ cup all-purpose flour
1 teaspoon Kashmiri red chile powder
1 teaspoon garlic powder
1 teaspoon onion powder
½ teaspoon salt
¼ teaspoon cayenne
¼ teaspoon ground cumin
¼ teaspoon smoked paprika
Black pepper, to taste
½ cup plus 2 tablespoons water

dry batter
½ cup all-purpose flour
½ cup panko breadcrumbs
1 teaspoon Kashmiri red chile powder
1 teaspoon garlic powder
1 teaspoon onion powder
1 teaspoon salt
¼ teaspoon cayenne
¼ teaspoon ground cumin
¼ teaspoon smoked paprika
Black pepper, to taste

harissa lime aioli
3 tablespoons mayonnaise
1 tablespoon harissa paste
1 teaspoon lime juice

for serving
1 burger bun
Romaine lettuce leaves
Sliced tomatoes
Thinly sliced red onions
Pickles

buffalo burgers

serves 2

I promise no buffaloes were harmed in the making of this burger. Instead, this comfort classic turned meatless is full of juicy tofu goodness. Use The Best Frozen Tofu Technique (page 39) to amp up the texture and create that perfect bite.

1. For the best flavor, prepare the tofu using The Best Frozen Tofu Technique (page 39). Otherwise, drain the tofu, wrap in paper towels, and press under a heavy pot or pan for 15 minutes to remove the excess water.

2. Cut the tofu horizontally into two slabs. I like to cut each slab into a long oval shape, resembling a chicken breast, by cutting off the corners.

3. Create a batter station. **Make the wet batter:** Whisk together the flour, chile powder, garlic powder, onion powder, salt, and water in a medium shallow bowl until no lumps remain.

4. **Make the dry batter:** Mix together the flour, panko breadcrumbs, chile powder, garlic powder, onion powder, and salt in a separate medium shallow bowl.

5. Evenly coat each slab of tofu in the wet batter, let the excess drip off, and then gently place the tofu into the dry batter and coat evenly on both sides. Gently press the dry batter into the tofu so it adheres well.

6. Heat about 1 inch of oil in a heavy medium skillet over medium heat. Gently place the tofu slabs, one at a time, into the skillet and cook until crispy and golden brown, about 5 minutes.

7. Remove the tofu from the skillet. Let cool on a paper towel-lined plate.

8. **Make the Buffalo sauce:** Place the butter in a small bowl and microwave in 15-second intervals until it melts. Add the hot sauce and whisk together.

9. Using a basting brush, evenly coat the tofu in the sauce.

10. To assemble the burgers, divide the tofu between the buns. Top with lettuce, tomato, pickles, and ranch dressing, and serve.

- One 16-ounce block extra-firm tofu
- Canola oil, for frying

wet batter
- ½ cup all-purpose flour
- ½ teaspoon Kashmiri red chile powder
- ½ teaspoon garlic powder
- ½ teaspoon onion powder
- ½ teaspoon salt
- 1¼ cups water

dry batter
- ½ cup all-purpose flour
- ½ cup Japanese-style panko breadcrumbs
- ½ teaspoon Kashmiri chile powder
- ½ teaspoon garlic powder
- ½ teaspoon onion powder
- ½ teaspoon salt

buffalo sauce
- 2 to 3 tablespoons unsalted butter
- ½ cup Frank's RedHot sauce

for serving
- 2 sesame seed hamburger buns, toasted
- Iceberg lettuce
- Tomato slices
- Sandwich pickle chips
- Ranch dressing

make it meatless

buffalo chicken snack wraps

serves 2

I think eating a wrap with a cold tortilla should be a jail-able offense, so for this Buffalo wrap, we're gently warming the tortillas (as God intended) before adding the crispy Buffalo chicken, cheddar, lettuce, and ranch dressing.

1. Break the mushrooms for the Classic Fried Chicken into about 12 bite-size pieces. Proceed with step 3 of that recipe and then reduce the frying time to 3 to 4 minutes in step 5. (The smaller pieces will fry more quickly.) No need to include the fresh squeeze of lemon at the end.

2. **Make the Buffalo sauce:** Combine the hot sauce, butter, cayenne, and paprika in a medium bowl.

3. Add the chicken to the buffalo sauce and toss to coat.

4. Heat a medium skillet over medium heat. Warm the tortillas, one at a time, for about 30 seconds per side.

5. To assemble the snack wraps, divide the chicken strips between the tortillas and then add cheddar, lettuce, and ranch dressing. Roll the wraps, and serve.

1 batch Classic Fried Chicken (page 27), prepared through step 2

buffalo sauce
½ cup Frank's RedHot sauce
2 tablespoons unsalted butter, melted
⅛ teaspoon cayenne
⅛ teaspoon smoked paprika

for serving
2 large flour tortillas
¼ cup shredded cheddar
½ cup shredded romaine lettuce
Ranch dressing, to taste

burgers & sandwiches

pulled pork sandwiches

serves 2

These shredded, smoky-sweet, seasoned oyster mushrooms mimic the texture of classic pulled pork for the perfect bite!

1. Hold one mushroom by the cap and use a fork to shred the body of the mushroom. Repeat with the second mushroom.

2. Combine the oil, soy sauce, ponzu sauce, liquid smoke, garlic powder, onion powder, and paprika in a medium bowl. Add a light sprinkling of salt and pepper to taste.

3. Add the mushrooms, and use your hands to massage the sauce into the mushrooms to evenly coat. Let marinate at room temperature for 1 hour.

4. Preheat the oven to 450°F.

5. Spread the mushrooms on a large baking sheet, ensuring there is plenty of space between the pieces. Roast for 7 to 10 minutes, until the edges are crispy but the mushrooms aren't burnt. Remove the mushrooms from the oven. Let cool at room temperature for about 5 minutes.

6. Add the barbecue sauce and toss to coat evenly.

7. Evenly divide the mushrooms between the buns. Top with buttermilk ranch dressing, and serve with coleslaw on the side.

2 large king oyster mushrooms (about 8 ounces)
2 tablespoons olive oil
1 tablespoon dark soy sauce
2 teaspoons ponzu sauce
1 teaspoon mesquite liquid smoke
½ teaspoon garlic powder
½ teaspoon onion powder
¼ teaspoon smoked paprika
Salt and black pepper, to taste
¼ cup barbecue sauce (I like Sweet Baby Ray's Sweet 'n Spicy)

for serving
2 sesame seed buns
Buttermilk ranch dressing
Coleslaw

crispy fish sandwiches
with tartar sauce
serves 2

Banana blossoms are a very common fish substitute, but if they're not your thing, enoki mushrooms provide the perfect fishy flavor for recreating your favorite seafood recipes. Here, the shrooms are coated in a light and airy batter, fried to golden brown perfection, and then topped off with a homemade tartar sauce.

1 **Make the batter:** With the fishy batter in a medium bowl, add the chile powder, garlic powder, onion powder, paprika, and pepper, and mix well.

2 **Make the fish:** Cut the ends (1 to 2 inches) off the enoki mushrooms, and discard them. Coat the mushrooms evenly in the batter. Divide the mushrooms in half, and clump them together in two separate portions.

3 Heat about 4 inches of canola oil (enough to submerge the mushrooms) in a small pot over medium heat.

4 Deep-fry the mushrooms until crispy and golden brown, about 5 minutes.

5 To assemble the burgers, divide the American cheese, lettuce, and mushrooms between the buns. Add plenty of tartar sauce, and serve.

batter
1 batch Fishy Batter (see Marinated and Battered Fish, page 36)
½ teaspoon Kashmiri red chile powder
¼ teaspoon garlic powder
¼ teaspoon onion powder
⅛ teaspoon smoked paprika
Black pepper, to taste

fish
7 ounces enoki mushrooms
Canola oil, for frying

for serving
2 slices American cheese
Romaine lettuce
2 brioche buns, toasted
Tartar Sauce (page 247)

pesto caprese sandwiches

serves 3

This cheesy pesto chicken sandwich is about to become a regular in your weeknight dinner rotation–I can feel it! An easy, fresh pesto is tossed onto toasty ciabatta rolls with seitan chicken, fresh mozzarella, and sun-dried tomatoes. Plus, we're adding my secret sandwich weapon: homemade spicy pickled onions.

1. **The day before you want to make the sandwiches, make the pickled red onions:** Heat a small pot over medium heat. Add the water, vinegar, sugar, chile, garlic, peppercorns, and salt. Bring to a soft boil, and cook, stirring, until the sugar and salt dissolve, about 1 minute.

2. Place the onion in a small mason jar or heatproof airtight container, and pour in the hot liquid. Let the mixture cool to room temperature, cover, and set in the refrigerator to pickle overnight.

3. The next day, preheat an air fryer to 400°F.

4. **Make the pesto:** Place the basil, oil, Parmesan, pine nuts, lemon juice, salt, and pepper in a food processor or blender, and blend to form a smooth paste, about 30 seconds.

5. **Cook the chicken:** Break the chicken into bite-size pieces. Heat the oil in a small skillet over medium heat. Add the chicken, season with salt and pepper, and sauté until slightly browned, 2 to 3 minutes.

6. To assemble the sandwiches, spread the pesto on the bottom halves of the rolls, then place the mozzarella, sun-dried tomatoes, and chicken on top.

7. Place the open-faced sandwiches and the tops of the rolls in the air fryer and bake for 5 minutes.

8. Add pickled onions to each sandwich, followed by the tops of the rolls to make three sandwiches. Serve.

pickled red onions
2 cups water
2 cups white vinegar
¼ cup sugar
1 large red chile, sliced
5 garlic cloves, sliced
1 tablespoon black peppercorns
2 teaspoons salt
1 large red onion, thinly sliced

pesto
3 ounces basil leaves
½ cup olive oil
¼ cup shredded Parmesan
¼ cup pine nuts
1 tablespoon lemon juice
¼ teaspoon salt
¼ teaspoon black pepper, or to taste

chicken
¼ batch Chicken 2.0 (page 21; see Note)
2 tablespoons olive oil
Salt and black pepper, to taste

for serving
3 ciabatta rolls or rolls of choice, sliced in half and toasted
6 slices fresh mozzarella
6 sun-dried tomatoes

note

If you're preparing only a quarter of a batch of the Chicken 2.0 for this recipe, reduce the steaming time to 35 to 40 minutes.

make it meatless

philly cheesesteaks

serves 2

I don't know much about Philadelphia besides the fact that (1) it's where the US Constitution was signed and (2) they make a killer cheesesteak sando–the important things. This one uses my meatless Beef (page 28) and melty provolone to reinvent the classic.

1. Heat the oil in a small skillet over medium heat. Add the onion, and sauté until translucent, 2 to 3 minutes.

2. Add the beef, oregano, salt, and pepper, and sauté until the beef is slightly browned, 2 to 3 minutes.

3. Turn off the heat, and cover the beef with the provolone. Cover the skillet, and let sit until the cheese melts, about 3 minutes.

4. To assemble the cheesesteaks, divide the cheesy beef mixture between the rolls, and serve.

- 1 tablespoon olive oil
- ¼ large yellow onion, chopped (about ¼ cup)
- ¼ batch Beef (page 28; see Note), sliced into thin strips
- ¼ teaspoon dried oregano
- Salt and black pepper, to taste
- 4 slices provolone
- 2 hoagie rolls, sliced in half and toasted

note

If you're preparing only a quarter of a batch of the Beef for this recipe, reduce the cooking time to 25 to 30 minutes.

burgers & sandwiches

Everyone's second favorite type of noods—these extra-meaty noodle dishes taste just like the real thing.

noods

chicken pad thai

serves 2

Let's play "never have I ever." I'll go first: Never have I ever made more attempts at a sauce recipe than I did for this pad Thai. Am I the only one with my hand raised? Recreating the perfect balance of savory, sweet, spicy, and tangy in a fish sauce-free pad Thai sauce was one of my life's missions, and I finally cracked the code with this recipe.

1. Cook the rice noodles according to the package instructions, and drain.

2. **Make the sauce:** Pour the water into a small bowl. Add the tamarind, and let sit for 30 minutes. Add the soy sauce, maple syrup, sriracha, lime juice, and red pepper flakes, and combine.

3. Heat the oil in a medium skillet over high heat. Add the shallot, and sauté until fragrant, about 30 seconds. Add the garlic, and sauté for another 30 seconds.

4. Add the cabbage, carrot, and chicken, and stir-fry for 2 to 3 minutes. The veggies should remain bright and crisp.

5. Add the sauce and the noodles, and stir to coat. Stir-fry for another 2 to 3 minutes to heat through.

6. Garnish with peanuts, bean sprouts, and cilantro, and serve.

8 ounces flat rice noodles
1½ tablespoons canola oil
½ shallot, thinly sliced
2 tablespoons chopped garlic
¼ cup shredded red cabbage
2 tablespoons shredded carrot
½ batch Chicken 3.0 (page 24; see Note), torn into bite-size pieces

pad thai sauce
2 tablespoons hot water
1 teaspoon fresh tamarind
3 tablespoons soy sauce
3 tablespoons maple syrup
2 tablespoons sriracha
1 teaspoon lime juice
1 teaspoon red pepper flakes

for serving
Peanuts
Bean sprouts
Chopped fresh cilantro

note

If you're preparing only half of a batch of the Chicken 3.0 for this recipe, reduce the cooking time to about 1 hour.

pad kee mao

serves 2

I love sending people noods, especially when they're covered in a sweet and savory sauce! How's that for a mental image? This dish is made with fresh and chewy rice noodles that are stir-fried with Chinese broccoli stems, red bell peppers, Roma tomatoes, and bamboo shoots. We're subbing in vegetarian oyster sauce for regular oyster sauce, and truly, you won't be able to tell the difference.

1 **Make the sauce:** Mix the brown sugar, water, oyster sauce, dark soy sauce, light soy sauce, and lime juice in a large bowl. Set aside.

2 **Make the rice noodles:** Place the noodles on a plate, and microwave for 30 seconds. (This will help them separate.) Gently pull apart the noodles and set them aside.

3 Heat a large, heavy skillet or wok over medium-high heat. Add the oil, shallot, and garlic, and cook, stirring constantly to prevent them from burning, for about 30 seconds.

4 Increase the heat to high. Add the broccoli stems and leaves, tomato, bell pepper, chile, and bamboo shoots, and stir-fry until the veggies start to soften slightly, 3 to 5 minutes. The veggies should remain crisp and bright.

5 Reduce the heat to medium. Add the noodles and ¼ cup of the sauce, and stir-fry until the sauce is well absorbed into the noodles and veggies, about 3 minutes.

6 Add more sauce if desired, and cook until the sauce is well absorbed. (Store the rest of the sauce in an airtight container in the refrigerator for later use, for up to 3 days.) Serve.

sauce
- ¼ cup brown sugar, firmly packed
- ¼ cup water
- 3 tablespoons vegetarian oyster sauce (I like Wan Ja Shan)
- 2 tablespoons dark soy sauce
- 2 tablespoons light soy sauce
- Juice of ½ lime

noodles
- 1 pound fresh wide rice noodles
- 3 tablespoons canola oil
- ½ shallot, finely chopped
- 4 garlic cloves, finely chopped
- 4 stems Chinese broccoli, halved lengthwise and leaves separated
- 1 Roma tomato, quartered
- ¼ red bell pepper, ribs and seeds removed, and sliced
- 1 Thai red chile, chopped, or to taste
- 1 tablespoon canned sliced bamboo shoots

note

You can add a quarter of a batch of Chicken 2.0 (page 21), torn into bite-size pieces, to this recipe if desired! Just reduce the steaming time to 35 to 40 minutes. Add it in step 4 with the veggies while stir-frying.

creamy sun-dried tomato pasta
with lemon-caper scallops

serves 2

A rich, decadent, creamy pasta is paired with light and fragrant lemony king oyster mushroom "scallops." That's a match made in heaven if you ask me.

1 **Make the pasta:** Bring a large pot of salted water to a boil over high heat. Add the bucatini, and cook according to the package instructions until al dente.

2 Meanwhile, heat the oil in a large skillet over medium heat. Add the shallot, and sauté until translucent, 1 to 2 minutes. Add the sun-dried tomatoes, garlic, and red pepper flakes, and sauté until fragrant, 1 to 2 minutes.

3 Reduce the heat to low. Add the Parmesan and heavy cream, and stir until the cheese has melted.

4 Add the vegetable broth and salt and pepper to taste, and simmer, stirring to combine, about 2 minutes.

5 Add the pasta to the pan with the sauce. Cook until the sauce thickens, about 3 more minutes.

6 **Make the scallops:** Cut the mushroom into 1-inch-thick discs.

7 Heat the butter in a heavy skillet over medium-low heat. Add the mushroom slices, sprinkle lightly with salt and pepper to taste, and sear the mushrooms until golden brown, 2 minutes per side. Add the capers, and sauté for 1 more minute.

8 Add the lemon juice and fresh dill, and turn off the heat. Baste the mushrooms with the butter sauce.

9 Serve the scallops on top of the pasta, and drizzle the butter sauce over the scallops right before serving.

pasta
8 ounces bucatini
2 tablespoons olive oil
1 shallot, chopped
2 tablespoons sun-dried tomatoes in olive oil, chopped
6 garlic cloves, finely chopped
1 teaspoon red pepper flakes
1 cup grated Parmesan, tightly packed
½ cup heavy cream
¾ cup vegetable broth
Salt and black pepper, to taste

scallops
2 large king oyster mushrooms
4 tablespoons salted butter
Salt and black pepper, to taste
1 tablespoon capers
1 tablespoon fresh lemon juice
3 fresh dill sprigs, chopped (about 2 packed teaspoons)

how to sear scallops

make it meatless

tan tan ramen

serves 2

Not to brag, but someone told me this is the best vegetarian ramen they've ever tried. This recipe uses many of the sauces and pastes (like spicy bean paste, sesame paste, and chili oil) found in traditional tan tan ramen to make a rich and flavorful broth. But to make it vegetarian (and vegan) friendly, we're using textured vegetable protein (TVP) and vital wheat gluten to recreate the texture of minced pork. The tare, a rich, concentrated mixture of sauces, adds depth of flavor to the hearty broth.

1. **Make the pork:** Place the TVP and hot water in a medium bowl, and mix until evenly combined. Let rest until the water is absorbed into the TVP, 5 minutes.

2. Sprinkle the vital wheat gluten over the TVP mixture, and gently toss the mixture with your hands until the TVP is evenly coated in the vital wheat gluten.

3. Heat the oil in a small skillet over medium heat. Add the TVP mixture, and sauté until the crumbles brown and start to crisp, 5 minutes.

4. Add the soy sauce, mirin, doubanjiang, ginger, garlic, brown sugar, liquid smoke, and paprika. Sauté until the sauces are absorbed into the TVP, 5 minutes.

5. **Make the broth:** Heat a medium pot over medium heat. Add the soy milk, water, bouillon paste, and brown sugar, and mix well. Bring to a soft boil and then immediately turn off the heat. (You don't want the soy milk to curdle.)

6. **Make the tare:** Mix the sesame paste, soy sauce, mirin, chili oil, and white miso paste in a small bowl.

7. Divide the tare between two serving bowls. Divide the broth between the bowls, and mix until the tare is evenly incorporated. Add half of the ramen noodles and pork to each bowl, and squeeze fresh lime juice on top of both.

8. **Make the drizzle:** Place the peanut butter, sriracha, and lime juice in a small bowl, and stir to combine. Drizzle half of this mixture over each serving bowl.

9. Garnish with soft-boiled eggs, bok choy, pickled ginger, scallions, and toasted seaweed, if using, and serve.

Two 3-ounce packets ramen noodles, cooked
Juice of 1 lime

pork
⅔ cup textured vegetable protein (TVP)
⅔ cup hot water
3 tablespoons vital wheat gluten (I recommend Anthony's)
6 tablespoons canola oil
2 tablespoons soy sauce
2 teaspoons mirin
2 tablespoons doubanjiang (spicy bean paste)
1 tablespoon roughly chopped ginger
3 garlic cloves, finely chopped
1 teaspoon brown sugar
½ teaspoon liquid smoke
¼ teaspoon smoked paprika

broth
2 cups unsweetened soy milk
2 cups water
1½ tablespoons vegetable bouillon paste
2 teaspoons brown sugar

tare
2 tablespoons sesame paste
2 tablespoons soy sauce
2 teaspoons mirin
1 teaspoon chili oil
1 teaspoon white miso paste

drizzle
1 tablespoon smooth peanut butter
1 tablespoon sriracha
Juice of 1 lime

for serving, optional
Marinated soft-boiled eggs
Blanched bok choy
Pickled ginger
Scallions
Toasted seaweed

sausage rigatoni

serves 1

If you're trying to learn how to cook, the perfect way to start is by mastering a few pasta sauces. This sausage rigatoni is a staple in my kitchen in part because it requires limited ingredients and basic skills. (This is the one time we're actually gonna love being basic.)

1 Bring a small pot of salted water to a boil over high heat. Add the rigatoni, and cook according to the package instructions until al dente. Drain, reserving ½ cup pasta water.

2 Heat the oil in a large skillet over medium heat. Add the onion, and sauté until translucent, about 1 minute. Add the garlic, and sauté for another 30 seconds.

3 Reduce the heat to low, and add the red pepper flakes, oregano, salt, and pepper. Sauté for about 1 minute.

4 Increase the heat to medium, add the tomato paste and bouillon paste, and sauté until the oil starts to separate slightly from the tomato paste, 2 to 3 minutes.

5 Add the pasta water, Parmesan, sausage, and heavy cream. Stir constantly until the Parmesan emulsifies in the sauce, 3 to 5 minutes.

6 Stir in the spinach, basil, and cooked pasta. Let the pasta cook in the sauce for about 2 minutes, and serve.

3 ounces rigatoni (1 cup)
3 tablespoons olive oil
½ medium yellow onion, chopped
2 tablespoons roughly chopped garlic
1 teaspoon red pepper flakes
½ teaspoon dried oregano
Salt and black pepper, to taste
3 tablespoons tomato paste
½ teaspoon vegetable bouillon paste
½ cup shredded Parmesan
½ cup Sausage Crumbles (page 31)
¼ cup heavy cream
Small handful baby spinach
4 to 6 large fresh basil leaves

make it meatless

bucatini carbonara

serves 2 to 4

Carbonara is famously meaty and creamy, and the traditional version includes guanciale, a fatty cut of pork jowl. My carbonara is just as creamy and cheesy, but I sub in meaty oyster mushroom bacon bits for the guanciale for a perfectly meatless version.

1½ cups freshly grated Parmesan, plus more for serving
2 eggs
1 egg yolk
2 large garlic cloves, minced
¾ teaspoon ground black pepper
Salt, to taste
6.5 ounces bucatini
1 tablespoon olive oil
1 batch Bacon Bits (see page 38)
Red pepper flakes, for garnish, optional

1. Place the Parmesan, eggs, egg yolk, garlic, pepper, and salt in a small bowl, and whisk together to form a fine paste.

2. Bring a medium pot of salted water to a boil over high heat. Add the bucatini, and cook according to the package instructions until al dente. Drain, reserving ¾ cup of the pasta water.

3. Heat the oil in a medium skillet over medium heat. Add the bacon bits, and cook until they are golden brown and the edges are crispy, 2 to 3 minutes.

4. Add the bucatini, pasta water, and cheese mixture, turn off the heat, and mix with a wooden spoon until everything emulsifies, 1 to 2 minutes. (The sauce should be silky and smooth, and the residual heat from the pan should be enough to cook the mixture.)

5. Garnish with red pepper flakes and more Parmesan, and serve.

chicken chow mein
serves 2

Noods should always be done tastefully. Sometimes, less is more. So we're getting back to basics with this one and making a classic chicken chow mien. It has soft noods, crisp veggies, and the perfect savory sauce combo with a little hint of sweetness for balance.

1. Combine the oyster sauce, light soy sauce, dark soy sauce, sesame oil, brown sugar, rice vinegar, salt, and white pepper in a small bowl.

2. Transfer half of the mixture to another small bowl, and add the water. Tear the lion's mane mushrooms into bite-size pieces, and add them to the bowl. Let them marinate at room temperature for about 1 hour. Reserve the other half of the sauce.

3. Wrap the marinated lion's mane in a paper towel and squeeze out as much moisture as possible. Discard the marinade.

4. Heat the oil in a large skillet over medium-high heat. Add the onion, and sauté for about 30 seconds. Add the cabbage and carrot. Increase the heat to high, and stir-fry for 2 minutes. The veggies should remain bright and crisp. Move the veggies to one side of the skillet.

5. Reduce the heat to medium, and add the lion's mane pieces to the empty side of the skillet. Stir-fry until the lion's mane pieces start to crisp up, 1 to 2 minutes.

6. Cook the chow mein noodles according to the package instructions and then transfer them to the skillet. Add the reserved sauce, and stir-fry until the ingredients are evenly combined, about 30 seconds.

7. Add the bean sprouts and scallions, and stir-fry until the bean sprouts just begin to soften slightly, about 1 minute. Serve.

- ¼ cup vegetarian oyster sauce (I like Wan Ja Shan)
- 3 tablespoons light soy sauce
- 2 tablespoons dark soy sauce
- 1 tablespoon plus 1 teaspoon sesame oil
- 2 teaspoons brown sugar
- 2 teaspoons rice vinegar
- 1 teaspoon salt
- ½ teaspoon white pepper
- ¼ cup water
- 4 ounces lion's mane mushrooms
- 2 tablespoons canola oil
- ¼ large red onion, thinly sliced
- 1 cup shredded green cabbage
- ½ cup shredded carrot
- 3.5 ounces dry chow mein noodles
- ¾ cup bean sprouts
- ¼ cup scallions, chopped

street

food

This ode to street food contains recipes that satisfy your cravings without breaking the bank.

korean corn dogs

makes 4 corn dogs

Nothing brings me more joy than a good mozzarella pull, so these Korean Corn Dogs are certainly a mood booster. This popular Korean street food has many variations, but here we're making a classic version with hot dogs and mozzarella fried in a crispy panko breadcrumb batter. (Or you can ditch the dogs altogether and skewer plain cheese sticks instead! Just cut a block of low-moisture mozzarella lengthwise into ¾-inch sticks.) You can also add crumbled crunchy Flamin' Hot Cheetos to the batter instead of panko breadcrumbs, but you didn't hear it from me.

1 **Make the batter:** Mix the water, sugar, and yeast in a glass. Let sit at room temperature until frothy on top, 5 to 10 minutes.

2 Whisk together the all-purpose flour, glutinous rice flour, and salt in a large bowl. Add the yeast mixture, and mix with a spatula. The batter will be very wet and sticky.

3 Cover the bowl with a damp cloth, and let the dough rise at room temperature for 1 hour.

4 Line a baking sheet with parchment paper.

5 **Make the filling:** Place the hot dogs on skewers, and wrap a slice of mozzarella around each one. Use the warmth of your hands to slightly melt the cheese and press the edges closed. Place the corn dogs, cheese seam side down, on the baking sheet. Set in the freezer for 30 minutes to help set the cheese.

6 Spread the panko breadcrumbs on a plate.

7 Dip the skewered hot dogs into the batter and cover evenly. (You may need to use a silicone spatula to even out the batter.) Then dip the battered hot dogs in the panko breadcrumbs, making sure to coat evenly.

8 Heat a large skillet over medium heat. Add enough oil to submerge the corn dogs when they're laid on their sides, and heat to 350°F.

9 Deep-fry the corn dogs until crispy and golden brown, 3 to 5 minutes, using tongs to flip and turn them as needed to ensure they cook evenly.

10 Serve with ketchup, Kewpie mayo, and mustard or your condiments of choice.

batter
- 1¼ cups warm water
- 2 tablespoons sugar
- One 0.25-ounce packet active dry yeast
- 1⅔ cups all-purpose flour
- ⅓ cup glutinous rice flour
- 1 teaspoon salt
- 1 cup Japanese-style panko breadcrumbs

filling
- 1 batch Hot Dogs (page 30)
- 4 slices low-moisture, part-skim mozzarella (see Note)
- Canola oil, for frying

for serving
Ketchup
Kewpie mayonnaise
Mustard

note

For extra cheese pull, you can double the mozzarella slices (two per hot dog).

make it meatless

carnitas tacos
serves 2

If you don't like jackfruit as a meat substitute, I will no longer be trusting your opinions on any other matters. (Sorry.) These jackfruit carnitas are perfectly seasoned and satisfying with the right hint of smokiness. Plus, this filling doesn't have to be used for just tacos; you can add it to quesadillas and burritos, too. We love versatility.

1. Drain the jackfruit and then wrap it in a few paper towels or a clean kitchen towel. Squeeze out as much liquid as you can over the sink. Pull apart the jackfruit pieces into "shreds."

2. Heat a medium skillet over medium heat. Add the oil. Then add the onion, garlic, and jalapeño, and sauté until the mixture is fragrant and the onions are slightly translucent, 1 to 2 minutes.

3. Add the jackfruit, and sauté until the excess moisture evaporates, about 2 minutes.

4. Add the vegetable broth, lime juice, orange juice, soy sauce, liquid smoke, chili powder, cumin, oregano, salt, and pepper. Increase the heat to medium-high, and sauté until the liquid is absorbed, about 5 minutes.

5. Warm the tortillas in a medium skillet over medium heat, about 15 seconds per side.

6. Evenly divide the carnitas among the tortillas, garnish with chopped onion and cilantro, and serve with lime wedges on the side.

One 14-ounce can young green jackfruit
2 tablespoons canola oil
¼ medium yellow onion, chopped
2 large garlic cloves, finely chopped
½ jalapeño, finely chopped
¼ cup vegetable broth
Juice of ½ lime
2 teaspoons fresh navel orange juice
1½ teaspoons dark soy sauce
½ teaspoon liquid smoke
½ teaspoon chili powder
½ teaspoon ground cumin
½ teaspoon dried Mexican oregano
Salt and black pepper, to taste
6 to 8 soft corn tortillas

for serving
Chopped yellow onion
Chopped cilantro
Lime wedges

chicken fajitas

serves 4 to 6

I hate meal prepping, but I'll make an exception for these delicious chicken fajitas. They're simple, quick to prepare, and pack the right amount of kick. No more flavorless chicken and rice for you! You can thank me later.

1. Heat the oil in a medium skillet over high heat. Add the onion and bell peppers, and sauté until the veggies soften slightly, about 2 minutes. The bell peppers should remain vibrant.

2. Reduce the heat to low. Add the chili powder, cumin, oregano, garlic powder, onion powder, paprika, salt, and pepper. Add the lime juice, and sauté for about 1 minute.

3. Add the chicken, and sauté until all the ingredients are combined and the spices are evenly distributed, about 1 minute.

4. Warm the tortillas in another medium skillet over medium heat for about 15 seconds per side.

5. Evenly divide the chicken fajita mixture among the tortillas. Garnish with cilantro, and serve with lime wedges on the side.

¼ cup neutral oil (such as canola or vegetable)
1 medium yellow onion, thinly sliced
3 bell peppers (ideally orange, red, and green), ribs and seeds removed, and thinly sliced
1 tablespoon chili powder
2 teaspoons ground cumin
2 teaspoons dried Mexican oregano
1 teaspoon garlic powder
1 teaspoon onion powder
½ teaspoon smoked paprika
Salt and black pepper, to taste
Juice of 1 lime
1 batch Chicken 1.0 (page 20)
4 to 6 flour tortillas

for serving
Cilantro
Lime wedges

chili chicken

serves 4

Before you start dialing 911 because I used ketchup in this recipe, hear me out. Ketchup is commonly used as a base in a variety of Asian cuisines (especially in Indo-Chinese recipes), and trust me, it's delicious. At its essence, ketchup is just tomatoes, sugar, and vinegar, so really, I promise you, it's not that weird. Cooking the ketchup in the oil reduces its tartness, creating a rich base similar to other tomato sauces and pastes. Okay, that's it. That's the end of my ketchup TED Talk.

3 tablespoons canola oil
½ batch Chicken 2.0 (page 21), torn into bite-size pieces
½ shallot, finely chopped
¼ cup chopped scallions, plus more for serving
4 to 6 dried arbol chiles, broken and seeds removed, if desired, to reduce heat
3 large garlic cloves, minced
2 tablespoons ketchup
2 tablespoons soy sauce
2 tablespoons sriracha
1 tablespoon honey
2 teaspoons rice vinegar
1 teaspoon Kashmiri red chile powder
¼ teaspoon smoked paprika
⅛ teaspoon black pepper
5 drops red gel food coloring
¾ cup water
1 tablespoon cornstarch
Cooked rice, for serving

1 Heat the oil in a medium skillet over medium heat. Add the chicken, and lightly pan-fry until it starts to crisp up, 1 to 2 minutes. Transfer the chicken to a plate, and set aside.

2 Add the shallot to the skillet, and sauté until fragrant, about 1 minute. Add the scallions, chiles, and garlic, and sauté until fragrant, about 1 minute.

3 Add the ketchup, soy sauce, sriracha, honey, vinegar, chile powder, paprika, black pepper, and food coloring. Stir to combine and cook until the sauce begins to thicken, 2 to 3 minutes. The consistency should resemble ketchup.

4 Whisk together the water and cornstarch in a small bowl to form a smooth slurry.

5 Reduce the heat to low, add the slurry to the skillet, and combine. Let the sauce mixture simmer until it thickens to a gravy consistency, about 5 minutes.

6 Add the chicken to the sauce mixture, and mix well until the sauce is evenly distributed.

7 Serve the chicken over a bed of warm rice, and garnish with more scallions.

street food

birria tacos

serves 2

These birria tacos were one of the first dishes I made meatless! Granted, I've never actually tried real birria because I learned about this dish after I'd already been a vegetarian for years, but there's no denying that this recipe is out of this world. It includes a rich, fiery broth, meaty king oyster mushroom shreds, Oaxaca cheese, fresh cilantro, crisp chopped onions, and lots of fresh lime juice. Oof.

1. **Make the broth:** Heat the canola oil in a large pot over medium heat. Add the onion, and sauté until translucent, about 2 minutes. Add the garlic, and sauté until fragrant, 1 minute.

2. Add the cloves, salt, peppercorns, cumin, oregano, red chile powder, pasilla chile powder, and cinnamon. Sauté until fragrant, 1 more minute.

3. Add the tomatoes and their juice, then crush the tomatoes with a wooden spoon. Sauté until softened, about 5 minutes.

4. Add the water, broth, arbol chiles, California chiles, guajillo chiles, and bay leaves. Simmer over medium-low heat for about 1 hour.

5. Remove the bay leaves. Blend broth well with an immersion blender until the mixture is smooth.

6. **Make the meat:** Shred the king oyster mushrooms with a fork.

7. Heat the oil in a medium skillet over medium heat. Add the mushrooms, and sauté until all the water releases, about 5 minutes.

8. Evenly sprinkle the taco seasoning over top of the mushrooms, and sauté until fragrant, 1 more minute.

9. Transfer ⅓ cup of the birria broth to the pan with the mushrooms, and cook until the broth is fully absorbed, about 5 minutes.

10. To assemble, heat another medium skillet over medium heat. Dip the tortillas in the broth, coating on both sides. Cook the tortillas, three at a time, in the skillet until they are dry but not crispy, about 2 minutes per side.

11. With the tortillas still in the pan, add the mushrooms and cheese to half of each tortilla and then fold the other side of the tortilla over it. Use a spatula to press down on the tacos to help them heat evenly through the center so the cheese melts. Add a few extra tablespoons of broth to the pan as needed to ensure that, as the cheese melts, the tortillas stay crispy but not burnt. Repeat steps 10 and 11 with the remaining tortillas, mushrooms, and cheese.

12. Serve with chopped onion, cilantro, and a side of broth for dipping. Add a generous squeeze of lime.

broth
2 tablespoons canola oil
¼ large yellow onion, chopped
7 garlic cloves, chopped
4 whole cloves
1 teaspoon salt, or to taste
½ teaspoon black peppercorns
½ teaspoon ground cumin
½ teaspoon dried Mexican oregano
¼ teaspoon Kashmiri red chile powder
¼ teaspoon pasilla chile powder
⅛ teaspoon ground cinnamon
One 28-ounce can San Marzano tomatoes
5½ cups water
2½ cups vegetable broth
5 arbol chiles
2 California chiles
2 guajillo chiles
4 bay leaves

meat
8 ounces king oyster mushrooms
2 tablespoons canola oil
1 teaspoon taco seasoning

assembly
7 or 8 street taco flour tortillas
2 cups shredded Oaxaca cheese
Finely chopped yellow onion
Finely chopped fresh cilantro
Lime wedges

korean fried chicken bao

serves 6

A soft, delicate exterior with a crispy, firecracker filling. But enough about me. You should really try these bao. This recipe includes plush and fluffy bao buns filled with crispy deep-fried oyster mushroom chicken that gets coated in a rich and spicy gochujang sauce and is served alongside a tangy slaw.

buns
- 1¼ cups milk or oat milk
- 2 teaspoons sugar
- One 0.25-ounce packet active dry yeast
- 3 cups all-purpose flour
- 2 tablespoons salt
- 1 tablespoon baking powder
- ⅓ cup water
- Canola oil, for brushing

dry batter
- ⅓ cup all-purpose flour
- ⅓ cup potato starch
- 1 teaspoon garlic powder
- 1 teaspoon salt
- ½ teaspoon coarse gochugaru flakes
- ¼ teaspoon white pepper

wet batter
- ⅔ cup all-purpose flour
- 2 teaspoons garlic powder
- 2 teaspoons salt
- 1 teaspoon coarse gochugaru flakes
- ½ teaspoon white pepper
- ⅓ cup plus 1 tablespoon water

chicken
- 6 ounces oyster mushrooms
- Canola oil, for frying

sauce
- 2 tablespoons gochujang paste
- 1 tablespoon soy sauce
- 1 tablespoon ketchup
- 2 teaspoons honey
- 1 teaspoon coarse gochugaru flakes
- 1 teaspoon Dijon mustard
- 1 teaspoon rice vinegar
- ½ teaspoon sesame oil
- ¼ teaspoon minced garlic
- ¼ teaspoon minced ginger

slaw
- ¼ cup mayonnaise
- 1 teaspoon honey
- 1 teaspoon lemon juice
- ½ teaspoon coarse gochugaru flakes
- ½ teaspoon rice vinegar
- ½ teaspoon soy sauce
- ¼ teaspoon toasted sesame oil
- ⅛ teaspoon smoked paprika
- Salt and black pepper, to taste
- 1 cup shredded red cabbage

for serving, optional
- Microgreens
- Pickled daikon radish and carrots (see page 220)

1 **Make the buns:** Pour the milk into a large mug and microwave until warm, about 45 seconds.

2 Add the sugar and yeast, and mix well. Let the mixture sit at room temperature for about 10 minutes. (You may see some small bubbles on the surface as the yeast activates.)

3 Combine the flour, salt, and baking powder in a large bowl. Add the yeast mixture and the water, and knead, using your hands or a stand mixer with a dough hook attachment on medium-low speed, until the dough is well combined and soft, about 5 minutes.

4 Cover the bowl with a kitchen towel, and let the dough rest at room temperature until doubled in size and light and airy to the touch, about 1 hour.

5 Evenly divide the dough into 12 pieces (about 2 ounces each). Roll the dough pieces into balls and then flatten them with a rolling pin until they are about ½ inch thick. Lightly brush the dough pieces with a thin coat of oil, and gently fold them in half (do not press) to create a semicircle shape.

make it meatless

6 Set up a steamer basket: Select a pot wide enough for the steamer basket to rest inside without touching the water at the bottom. Fill the pot with 1 to 2 inches of water. (The basket should not be submerged in the water.) Line the basket with parchment paper, and place 3 to 5 buns on top, leaving some space in between. Do not overcrowd. Bring the water to a boil over high heat and then reduce the heat to medium-low. Cover and steam until the dough has increased in size, is springy to the touch, and has a little shine on the surface, 8 to 10 minutes. It should not be sticky.

7 Remove the buns from the steamer, and set aside to cool. Repeat the steaming process with the remaining buns.

8 Create a batter station. **Make the dry batter:** Combine the flour, potato starch, garlic powder, salt, gochugaru, and white pepper in a medium bowl.

9 **Make the wet batter:** Whisk together the flour, garlic powder, salt, gochugaru, white pepper, and water in another medium bowl until no clumps remain.

10 **Make the chicken:** Break the oyster mushrooms into 4 or 5 bite-size chunks. Generously coat the mushroom pieces in the wet batter, letting any excess batter drip off. Then gently toss the mushroom pieces in the dry batter until they are evenly coated.

11 Gently press the dry batter, 2 to 3 tablespoons at a time, into the wet batter until the mixture starts to slightly clump together. At first, the mixture will appear to dampen, but make sure to continue pressing until the outside layer appears dry. (You may not need to use all the dry batter.)

12 Heat enough canola oil to submerge the mushroom pieces in a large skillet over medium heat. Gently place the mushroom pieces into the oil, and cook until crispy and golden brown, 5 to 8 minutes. To ensure the batter will not fall off, do not flip or move them around in the pan for the first minute.

13 **Make the sauce:** Combine the gochujang, soy sauce, ketchup, honey, gochugaru, mustard, vinegar, sesame oil, garlic, and ginger in a small bowl. Coat the cooked mushroom pieces in the sauce.

14 **Make the slaw:** Combine the mayonnaise, honey, lemon juice, gochugaru, vinegar, soy sauce, sesame oil, paprika, salt, and pepper in a small bowl. Add the cabbage, and stir to coat.

15 Place the mushrooms inside the steamed buns. Garnish with the microgreens and pickled daikon and carrots, if desired, and serve with the slaw.

street food

soup,
curri
& ste

Recipes that feel like
a warm hug in a bowl.

thai chicken red curry

serves 2

This delicious Thai red curry softly balances sweet, savory, and earthy flavors. Fresh ginger, Thai basil, creamy coconut milk, and stalks of lemongrass create an aromatic and heartwarming dish you're sure to love.

1 Heat the oil in a medium pot over medium heat. Add the shallot, and sauté until translucent, about 2 minutes.

2 Add the bell peppers, garlic, and ginger, and sauté until fragrant, 1 to 2 minutes.

3 Reduce the heat to low. Add the curry paste and tomato paste, and sauté until the paste starts to separate from the oil, about 5 minutes.

4 Add the chicken, water, coconut milk, lemongrass, basil, bamboo shoots, soy sauce, brown sugar, bouillon paste, vinegar, salt, and pepper, and stir to combine.

5 Bring to a boil over high heat, then reduce the heat to low and simmer until thickened, 30 to 40 minutes. Remove the lemongrass and discard.

6 Garnish with cilantro, lime wedges, and Fresno chile slices, and serve over a bed of warm jasmine rice.

---

2 tablespoons canola oil
1 large shallot, finely chopped
2 small bell peppers (ideally red and green), ribs and seeds removed, and sliced
2 tablespoons chopped garlic
1½ tablespoons grated ginger
3 tablespoons Thai red curry paste
1 tablespoon plus 1 teaspoon tomato paste
½ batch Chicken 2.0 (page 21), torn into bite-size pieces
3 cups water
One 13.5-ounce can coconut milk
2 lemongrass stalks, ends removed
4 to 6 fresh Thai basil leaves
3 tablespoons sliced canned bamboo shoots, optional
1 tablespoon soy sauce
1 tablespoon brown sugar
2 teaspoons vegetable bouillon paste
2 teaspoons rice vinegar
Salt and black pepper, to taste

for serving
Chopped fresh cilantro
Lime wedges
Sliced Fresno chile
Cooked jasmine rice

make it meatless

chicken pho

serves 4

Every Seattleite knows that the start of rainy season means you've gotta grab the largest bowl of pho in your vicinity. During my sophomore year of college, I walked from campus to my favorite pho restaurant, Pho Tran, every. single. day. For nine months straight. I gave *food hyperfixation* a new meaning. I went through countless bottles of sriracha. I worried my peers. I just could not get enough! Sadly, Pho Tran has since closed, so I had to figure out how to make my own version at home.

1. Place a grill grate over the open flame on your stove (see Note 2). Place the onions and ginger on top, and char, using tongs to turn them, until they are blackened on all sides, 3 to 5 minutes. Carefully rinse the ginger under cool water and then roughly chop it.

2. Heat a large pot over medium heat. Add the canola oil, onion, ginger, garlic, coriander, green and black cardamom, cloves, star anise, and cinnamon. Toast until fragrant, about 2 minutes.

3. Add the water, celery, carrot, soy sauce, bouillon paste, vinegar, sugar, salt, nutritional yeast, and white pepper, and bring to a boil. Cover, reduce the heat to medium-low, and let simmer for about 1 hour.

4. Cook the pho noodles according to the package instructions, and drain.

5. Divide the broth among four serving bowls. Add the noodles and chicken. Garnish with the bean sprouts, basil, cilantro, lime wedges, shallots, sriracha, sambal, chili oil, and hoisin sauce, if using, and serve.

notes

1. If you're preparing only a quarter of a batch of the Chicken 2.0 for this recipe, reduce the steaming time to 35 to 40 minutes.

2. If you do not own a grill grate, you can use long tongs to hold the onions and ginger over the open flame until they're blackened. If you have an electric stove, you can use a griddle over medium-high or high heat.

- 2 small yellow onions, peeled and halved
- One 3-inch piece ginger
- 3 tablespoons canola oil
- 4 garlic cloves
- 3 teaspoons coriander seeds
- 2 green cardamom pods
- 1 large black cardamom pod
- 3 whole cloves
- 2 star anise pods
- One 2-inch cinnamon stick
- 3 quarts water
- 3 celery stalks, chopped
- 1 large carrot, chopped
- 2 tablespoons plus 1½ teaspoons soy sauce
- 1 tablespoon vegetable bouillon paste
- 1 tablespoon rice vinegar
- 2 teaspoons raw turbinado sugar
- 2 teaspoons salt, or to taste
- 1 teaspoon nutritional yeast
- ⅛ teaspoon white pepper
- 16 ounces pho noodles
- ¼ batch Chicken 2.0 (page 21; see Note 1), torn into bite-size pieces

for serving, optional
- Bean sprouts
- Fresh Thai basil
- Chopped fresh cilantro
- Lime wedges
- Thinly sliced shallot
- Sriracha
- Sambal
- Chili oil
- Hoisin sauce

soups, curries & stews

gumbo

serves 6

There are recipes that can warm your stomach, but only a hot bowl of gumbo can warm your soul. The base starts off with a lush, dark roux, and the stew itself is infused with classic Creole flavors that carefully balance salty, spicy, and sour notes.

1. Make a dark roux by heating the canola oil and flour in a large pot over low heat. Cook, stirring frequently, until the mixture turns a cinnamon brown color, 30 to 40 minutes. (Don't rush this step! This process gives the gumbo its complex toasty and nutty flavor.)

2. Heat the olive oil in a medium skillet over medium heat. Add the sausage, and sear until browned and the edges are crispy, about 5 minutes. Remove from the heat, and set aside.

3. Add the onion, celery, and bell pepper to the roux, and mix. Cook until everything is well coated, another 3 minutes.

4. Add the water, tomatoes, garlic, bay leaves, hot sauce, bouillon paste, Cajun seasoning, chili powder, paprika, thyme, salt, and pepper, and stir. Reduce the heat to low, and simmer for about 30 minutes.

5. Add the sausage, and simmer until the gumbo has thickened to a soup consistency, 10 to 15 minutes.

6. Remove the bay leaves and discard.

7. Before serving, add the gumbo filé and stir. Serve with warm rice and additional hot sauce, to taste.

---

1 cup canola oil
1 cup all-purpose flour
3 tablespoons olive oil
1 batch Sausage (page 31), sliced 1 inch thick
1 cup diced yellow onion
1 cup chopped celery
1 cup diced green bell pepper
8 cups water
One 14.5-ounce can diced tomatoes
2 tablespoons finely chopped garlic
6 bay leaves
2 tablespoons Louisiana hot sauce, plus more for serving
1 tablespoon vegetable bouillon paste
1 tablespoon Cajun seasoning
1 teaspoon chili powder
½ teaspoon smoked paprika
¼ teaspoon dried thyme
Salt and black pepper, to taste

for serving
2 teaspoons gumbo filé
Cooked rice

how to make the roux

102 make it meatless

italian meatball soup

serves 2 to 5

This hearty, tomato-y meatball soup is basically like Nonna's hugs in a bowl. Okay, maybe it's not quite that good, but it's pretty darn close.

1. Heat the oil in a large pot over medium heat. Add the onion, and sauté until translucent, 1 or 2 minutes. Add the garlic, and sauté until fragrant, 1 more minute. Add the Italian seasoning and red pepper flakes, and sauté for 1 minute.

2. Add the tomatoes, basil, salt, and pepper, and sauté until the tomatoes start to separate from the oil, 5 to 7 minutes.

3. Add the water, bouillon paste, and parsley. Increase the heat to high, and bring the mixture to a boil. Reduce the heat to low, and simmer until thickened, about 40 minutes.

4. Add the meatballs and ditalini, and simmer until the pasta is cooked through and the meatballs are evenly heated, 20 minutes.

5. Garnish with grated Parmesan and chopped fresh parsley, and serve.

3 tablespoons olive oil
1 medium yellow onion, chopped
3 tablespoons chopped garlic
2 teaspoons Italian seasoning
1 teaspoon red pepper flakes, or to taste
1 cup canned crushed tomatoes
6 large fresh basil leaves, roughly torn
Salt and black pepper, to taste
6 cups water
1 tablespoon vegetable bouillon paste
1 tablespoon chopped fresh parsley, plus more for serving
1 batch Italian Meatballs (page 34), refrigerated overnight
1 cup ditalini
Grated Parmesan, for serving

soups, curries & stews

chili

serves 4

This hearty chili is packed with meaty crumbles (thanks to the invention of textured vegetable protein!) and smothered in plenty of delicious toppings like cheddar cheese, sour cream, cilantro, onions, and crushed tortilla chips. It has wonderful textures, bold flavors, and the perfect amount of heat.

1. Heat the oil in a large pot over medium heat. Add the onion and bell peppers, and sauté until the veggies are tender and translucent, about 5 minutes.

2. Add the jalapeños and garlic, and sauté until fragrant, 3 to 5 minutes.

3. Add the tomato paste, and sauté until all the excess moisture is cooked out of the veggies, 3 to 5 minutes.

4. Add the beans, tomatoes, green chiles, chili powder, brown sugar, salt, cumin, oregano, paprika, cayenne, bay leaves, and water, and stir. Bring to a boil. Reduce the heat to medium-low, cover, and simmer, stirring periodically, for 1 hour. If the chili is too thick, add 1 more cup of water.

5. Add the meat crumbles, and simmer until the chili thickens to a dense, soup-like consistency, about 30 minutes.

6. Serve, topped with cheddar, sour cream, red onions, cilantro, and tortilla chips.

5 tablespoons olive oil
1 large yellow onion, finely chopped
2 bell peppers (ideally red and green), ribs and seeds removed, and diced
2 jalapeños, finely chopped
2 tablespoons finely chopped garlic
2 tablespoons tomato paste
Two 15.5-ounce cans dark red kidney beans, rinsed and drained
1¼ cups canned crushed tomatoes
2 tablespoons canned diced fire-roasted green chiles
1 to 2 tablespoons chili powder, to taste
1 tablespoon brown sugar
2 teaspoons salt, or to taste
1 teaspoon ground cumin
1 teaspoon dried oregano
½ teaspoon smoked paprika
¼ teaspoon cayenne
2 bay leaves
5 cups water
2 cups Meat Crumbles (page 33; see Note)

for serving
Shredded cheddar
Sour cream
Chopped red onions
Chopped fresh cilantro
Crushed tortilla chips

note

You can also crumble up Italian Meatballs (page 54) or Sausage (page 51) for this recipe in place of the meat crumbles.

106   **make it meatless**

snack
&

apps

Who said vegetarian food has to be complicated? Here are some quick and easy meatless snacks you can throw together without sacrificing flavor.

sesame scallops

serves 1

The versatility of mushrooms as meat really shines in this beautiful sweet, savory, and umami dish that uses king oyster mushroom to replicate scallops. A bonus: You can make more of this sauce and drizzle it into your weekly stir-fry.

1 large king oyster mushroom (4 to 5 ounces)
2 tablespoons honey
2 tablespoons soy sauce
1 teaspoon sesame oil
½ teaspoon red pepper flakes
¼ teaspoon cornstarch
1 tablespoon canola oil

for serving
Sesame seeds
Microgreens
Cooked jasmine rice, optional

1 Slice the mushroom into 1-inch-thick pieces.

2 Mix the honey, soy sauce, sesame oil, red pepper flakes, and cornstarch in a small bowl.

3 Heat the canola oil in a medium skillet over medium heat. Add the mushroom slices, making sure not to overcrowd the pan, and sear for 2 to 3 minutes per side.

4 Reduce the heat to low, and add the sauce. Cook the scallops in the sauce until they are browned and the edges are crispy, about 1 minute per side. Transfer the scallops to a plate.

5 Increase the heat to medium-high, and let the remaining sauce bubble and thicken for 20 seconds.

6 Stir well and then pour over the scallops. Garnish with sesame seeds and microgreens, and serve over a bed of warm rice, if using.

chicken nachos

serves 4

This is *na'cho* typical nacho recipe! (I know–I'll show myself out.) We're using Chicken 2.0 as the base and adding a silky-smooth cheese sauce, spicy chipotle drizzle, and plenty of toppings to make these hearty chicken nachos!

1. **Make the cheese sauce:** Heat the milk in a medium pot over low heat. Add the Velveeta, and gently whisk until the Velveeta melts and combines evenly with the milk, 5 to 7 minutes.

2. Add the Monterey Jack, chili powder, salt, cayenne, and paprika, and whisk until the Monterey Jack melts, 3 to 4 minutes.

3. Remove from the heat, add the jalapeño juice and hot sauce, and mix well.

4. **Make the chipotle drizzle:** Combine the jalapeño juice, chipotle peppers, and salt in a small bowl.

5. **Make the nachos:** Heat the oil in a medium skillet over medium heat. Add the chicken pieces, and sauté until lightly crispy and golden brown, 1 to 2 minutes.

6. To assemble, spread the tortilla chips over a large plate, and evenly layer the chicken pieces over the top. Cover with a generous amount of the cheese sauce, and top with the chipotle drizzle. Add the pico de gallo, crema, red onions, and cilantro, and serve.

cheese sauce
1 cup whole milk
16 ounces Velveeta, cubed
1 cup shredded Monterey Jack
1 teaspoon chili powder
½ teaspoon salt, or to taste
¼ teaspoon cayenne
⅛ teaspoon smoked paprika
2 tablespoons pickled jalapeño juice
Dash of hot sauce, or to taste

chipotle drizzle
3 tablespoons pickled jalapeño juice
2 tablespoons canned chipotle peppers in adobo sauce, blended
Salt, to taste

nachos
1 tablespoon canola oil
½ batch Chicken 2.0 (page 21), broken into bite-size pieces
One 15-ounce bag tortilla chips
Pico de gallo
Mexican crema
Diced red onions
Chopped fresh cilantro

snacks & apps

chipotle chicken tacos

makes 5 street tacos

A general rule of thumb for life: Chipotle sauce makes pretty much everything better. But especially these spicy chicken tacos.

1 Combine the blended chipotles, lime juice, garlic powder, onion powder, cumin, paprika, and salt in a small bowl.

2 Add the chicken, massage the marinade into the chicken pieces, and let marinate for about 5 minutes.

3 Heat 1 tablespoon canola oil in a medium skillet over medium heat. Add the chicken pieces, and sauté until crispy and golden brown, about 5 minutes.

4 **Make the pico de gallo:** Gently mix the tomatoes, onion, lime juice, olive oil, cilantro, salt, and pepper in a small bowl.

5 Heat the remaining 1 tablespoon canola oil in a medium skillet over medium heat. Add the tortillas, and fry for 30 to 60 seconds per side.

6 Assemble the tacos: With the tortillas still in the skillet, add the Monterey Jack and chicken to one half of each of the tortillas and fold them in half. Cook for another 30 to 60 seconds per side until the cheese melts.

7 Remove the tacos from the skillet. Add the chipotle sauce, pico de gallo, hot sauce, and shredded cabbage, and serve.

---

1 tablespoon canned chipotle peppers in adobo sauce, blended
Juice of ½ lime
½ teaspoon garlic powder
½ teaspoon onion powder
⅛ teaspoon ground cumin
⅛ teaspoon smoked paprika
Pinch of salt, or to taste
¼ batch Chicken 2.0 (page 21), broken into small pieces
2 tablespoons canola oil, divided
5 street taco flour tortillas

pico de gallo
2 Roma tomatoes, finely chopped
¼ small red onion, finely chopped
Juice of ½ lime
1 teaspoon olive oil
Chopped fresh cilantro, to taste
Salt and black pepper, to taste

for serving
⅔ cup shredded Monterey Jack
1 batch Chipotle Sauce (page 248)
Hot sauce (I recommend Valentina or Louisiana)
Shredded red cabbage, optional

---

note

If you're preparing only a quarter of a batch of the Chicken 2.0 for this recipe, reduce the steaming time to 35 to 40 minutes.

116   **make it meatless**

chicken taquitos

serves 6

These cheesy, crispy chicken taquitos are so rich, delicious, and flavorful! They're perfect for serving as a shareable snack or an appetizer at your next family gathering.

1. Place the cream cheese in a small bowl, and microwave for 10 seconds to soften. Transfer to a large bowl.

2. Add the cheddar, pepper jack, green chiles, lime juice, garlic powder, onion powder, chili powder, cumin, salt, and pepper, and mix well. Gently fold in the bell pepper and corn.

3. Heat the olive oil in a medium pan over medium heat. Add the chicken, and fry until golden brown, about 2 minutes. Remove the chicken, let cool for about 3 minutes, and then gently fold it into the cheese and vegetable mixture.

4. Heat 1 inch of canola oil in a large skillet over medium heat.

5. Divide the chicken mixture into six portions, place one portion in the middle of each tortilla, and roll the tortilla lengthwise. Working in two batches, carefully place the taquitos in the skillet, folded side down. Fry until the seams of the taquito bind together, about 2 minutes.

6. Flip over the taquitos and fry, using a chopstick, spatula, or tongs to hold down the folded end so the taquitos don't unravel, for 2 minutes.

7. Continue rotating and frying until the taquitos are golden brown, 3 to 5 minutes. Place on a paper towel–lined plate to remove any excess oil.

8. Serve with sour cream, hot sauce, pico de gallo, and chipotle sauce, if using.

note

If you're preparing only a quarter of a batch of the Chicken 2.0, reduce the cooking time to 35 to 40 minutes.

---

4 ounces cream cheese
1 cup shredded cheddar
½ cup shredded pepper jack
1 tablespoon canned diced fire-roasted green chiles
Juice of ½ lime
1 teaspoon garlic powder
1 teaspoon onion powder
1 teaspoon chili powder
½ teaspoon ground cumin
½ teaspoon salt
Black pepper, to taste
¼ cup chopped red bell pepper
¼ cup drained and rinsed canned corn
1 tablespoon olive oil
¼ batch Chicken 2.0 (page 21; see Note), torn into bite-size pieces
Canola oil, for frying
Six 6-inch flour tortillas

for serving, optional
Sour cream
Hot sauce
Pico de gallo
Chipotle Sauce (page 248)

snacks & apps

ceviche

serves 3 to 4

We're swapping out the seafood for meaty king oyster mushrooms in this bright and fresh ceviche. It's perfect for sharing as a quick and easy appetizer or as a light snack at your summer gatherings (or all year round, to be honest).

1 Set up a steamer basket: Place a metal steamer basket in a large pot. The steamer basket should be small enough to fit inside the pot with the lid closed. Add enough water to the pot to reach just below the steamer basket. (The basket should not be submerged in the water.) Bring the water to a boil over high heat and then reduce the heat to medium.

2 Add the mushrooms, cover, and steam until the mushrooms are tender, 5 minutes. Set aside, and let cool to room temperature.

3 Transfer the mushrooms to a large bowl. Add the tomatoes, onion, jalapeño, garlic, tomato juice, lime juice, and salt, and gently mix everything together.

4 Add the avocado, and gently mix again. (I leave this for the end so the avocado doesn't get mushy from being overmixed.)

5 Garnish with cilantro, and serve with tortilla chips.

---

2 king oyster mushrooms (about 12 ounces), diced

2 Roma tomatoes, chopped

¼ medium yellow onion, chopped

1 jalapeño, finely chopped

3 garlic cloves, chopped

½ cup tomato juice

Juice of 3 limes, or to taste

Himalayan salt, to taste

1 avocado, peeled, pitted, and chopped

Chopped fresh cilantro

Tortilla chips or tostadas, for serving

make it meatless

enchiladas
serves 4

These enchiladas are filled with cheesy, meaty crumbles and covered in a delicious homemade red enchilada sauce! This is the perfect dish to share at a family-style dinner (or to hoard for yourself–I'm not here to judge).

1. Preheat the oven to 350°F.

2. Heat ⅓ cup oil in a medium skillet over medium heat. Add the meat crumbles, and fry until they start to crisp up, about 5 minutes.

3. Add another ⅓ cup oil. Add the onion, jalapeño, salt, and pepper, and sauté until the crumbles are cooked through, crispy, and deep brown, 5 to 7 minutes.

4. **Make the enchilada sauce:** Melt the butter in a medium pot over medium heat. Reduce the heat to low, and add the flour, 1 tablespoon at a time, whisking vigorously to combine after each addition to make a roux. Cook the roux, whisking frequently, until it's a light golden brown, 2 to 3 minutes.

5. Add the chili powder, chipotle powder, garlic powder, onion powder, and oregano, and sauté for about 30 seconds. Add the tomato paste, tomato sauce, salt, and pepper. Use a spatula to break apart the tomato paste, and sauté for about 5 minutes.

6. Add the bouillon paste, vinegar, nutritional yeast, and water. Stir to combine, and simmer over low heat until the sauce thickens, 10 minutes.

7. Assemble the enchiladas: Add about half of the cheese blend and 1 cup enchilada sauce to the meat crumbles, and mix until evenly combined.

8. Working with one tortilla at a time, dip the tortillas into the enchilada sauce to coat both sides. Fill each tortilla with the meaty mixture, and roll up the tortilla. Place the filled enchiladas side by side in a 9 × 13-inch baking dish, and pour the remaining sauce on top. Sprinkle the remaining cheese over the top.

9. Bake for 12 to 18 minutes, until the cheese on top is nicely melted but the sauce is not dried out. Serve.

⅔ cup olive oil, divided
1 batch Meat Crumbles (page 33), prepared through step 3
1 small yellow onion, finely chopped
1 jalapeño, finely chopped
Salt and black pepper, to taste
8 ounces shredded Mexican cheese blend
6 large flour tortillas

enchilada sauce
3 tablespoons salted butter
3 tablespoons all-purpose flour
2 tablespoons chili powder
1 tablespoon chipotle powder
1 teaspoon garlic powder
1 teaspoon onion powder
¼ teaspoon dried Mexican oregano
¼ cup tomato paste
One 6-ounce can tomato sauce
Salt and black pepper, to taste
1½ tablespoons vegetable bouillon paste
1½ teaspoons apple cider vinegar
1 teaspoon nutritional yeast
3 cups water

snacks & apps

takeo

out

You can still enjoy all of your favorite take-out staples without meat. Let me show you!

teriyaki chicken

serves 2

I'm pretty sure you could fry a chopstick in this teriyaki sauce and it would taste good. That's how much I believe in this recipe. (Please don't do that though.) This sauce strikes the perfect balance between sweet, savory, and umami flavors, and it pairs perfectly with Chicken 3.0.

1 Combine the soy sauce, brown sugar, honey, sriracha, vinegar, sesame oil, and sesame seeds in a small bowl.

2 Create a cornstarch slurry by combining the cornstarch and water in another small bowl. Add the slurry to the sauce mixture, and mix well.

3 Transfer the sauce to a small saucepan, set over medium-low heat, and simmer, mixing continuously with a silicone spatula to prevent any clumping, until the sauce thickens slightly, 1 to 2 minutes.

4 Heat the canola oil in a medium skillet over medium heat. Add the chicken, and lightly pan-fry until it starts to crisp up, about 2 minutes.

5 Add the sauce to the skillet and stir to coat the chicken. Serve over a bed of warm rice, garnished with sesame seeds and scallions.

¼ cup soy sauce
3 tablespoons brown sugar
2 tablespoons honey
2 tablespoons sriracha
1 tablespoon rice vinegar
1 tablespoon sesame oil
1 teaspoon sesame seeds
1 tablespoon cornstarch
1 to 2 tablespoons water
1 to 2 tablespoons canola oil
½ batch Chicken 3.0 (page 24; see Note), broken into bite-size pieces

for serving
Cooked rice
Sesame seeds
Scallions

note

If you're preparing only half of a batch of the Chicken 3.0, reduce the cooking time to about 1 hour.

make it meatless

orange chicken

serves 2

The hardest thing about going plant-based, in whatever capacity, is feeling like you're missing out on your favorite take-out dishes. I hope by now you realize that isn't true! Especially when you're using vital wheat gluten; then, it's pretty easy. For this recipe, we'll be using Chicken 3.0, which I specially developed for sautéing *and* deep-frying! Seitan has the tendency to dry out if it's overcooked, but this chicken retains its moisture, even after deep-frying, making it perfect for this recipe. Plus, nothing can beat this fragrant savory and sweet sauce!

1 Create a batter station. **Make the dry batter:** Combine the flour, cornstarch, salt, chile powder, garlic powder, onion powder, cumin, and white pepper in a medium shallow bowl. **Then make the wet batter:** Whisk together the flour, chile powder, garlic powder, onion powder, salt, cumin, white pepper, and water in another medium shallow bowl until no lumps remain and the mixture resembles pancake batter.

2 **Make the chicken:** Coat the chicken first in the wet batter and then in the dry batter.

3 Heat enough canola oil to submerge the chicken in a medium pot over medium heat. Deep-fry the chicken until golden brown, 4 to 5 minutes. Transfer to a paper towel–lined plate.

4 **Make the sauce:** Whisk together the water and cornstarch in a medium bowl to create a cornstarch slurry.

5 Add the orange zest, orange juice, brown sugar, dark soy sauce, light soy sauce, vinegar, sesame oil, garlic, ginger, and paprika, and mix well.

6 Transfer the sauce to a small pot, and heat over medium heat until the mixture thickens to the consistency of maple syrup, gently bubbles, and the sugar dissolves, 3 to 5 minutes.

7 Add the chicken, and coat generously in the sauce.

8 Serve over a bed of warm rice, garnished with scallions and sesame seeds.

note

If you're preparing only half of a batch of the Chicken 3.0, reduce the cooking time to about 1 hour.

dry batter
1 cup all-purpose flour
1 tablespoon cornstarch
1 teaspoon salt
1 teaspoon Kashmiri red chile powder
1 teaspoon garlic powder
1 teaspoon onion powder
¼ teaspoon ground cumin
¼ teaspoon white pepper

wet batter
1 cup all-purpose flour
1 teaspoon Kashmiri red chile powder
1 teaspoon garlic powder
1 teaspoon onion powder
1 teaspoon salt
¼ teaspoon ground cumin
¼ teaspoon white pepper
1¼ cups water

chicken
½ batch Chicken 3.0 (page 24), torn into chunks
Canola oil, for frying

sauce
⅓ cup water
1 tablespoon cornstarch
Zest of ¼ navel orange
Juice of 1 navel orange
5 tablespoons brown sugar
1 tablespoon dark soy sauce
1 tablespoon light soy sauce
2 teaspoons rice vinegar
2 teaspoons toasted sesame oil
1 teaspoon minced garlic
¼ teaspoon minced ginger
¼ teaspoon smoked paprika

for serving
Cooked rice
Chopped scallions
Sesame seeds

takeout 131

chicken quesadilla

serves 2

These are like regular chicken quesadillas, but even more delicious, because we're adding a firecracker chipotle sauce in the center to make the melty cheese pull even better. (I know–I didn't think it was possible, either.)

1. Heat the oil in a medium saucepan over medium heat.

2. Sprinkle the chicken pieces evenly with the taco seasoning. Add to the pan, and stir-fry until lightly browned, about 2 minutes. Remove from the heat.

3. Add half of the chicken and half of the cheese to one half of each tortilla. Add the chipotle sauce, to taste, on top. Fold the quesadillas in half, and add them to the pan. Cover the pan with a lid to allow the steam to help melt the cheese in the center.

4. Let the quesadillas brown on the bottom, about 3 minutes, and then gently flip over. Brown on the other side, about another 3 minutes.

5. Serve with hot sauce and sour cream.

1 tablespoon canola oil
¼ batch Chicken 2.0 (page 21), torn into bite-size pieces
1 teaspoon taco seasoning
½ cup shredded Mexican cheese blend
2 large flour tortillas
Chipotle Sauce (page 248)

for serving
Hot sauce
Sour cream

note

If you're preparing only a quarter of a batch of the Chicken 2.0 for this recipe, reduce the steaming time to 35 to 40 minutes.

make it meatless

mongolian beef

serves 2

This popular Chinese American stir-fried dish contains tender and crispy beefless beef that's covered in a savory, tangy, and slightly sweetened sauce. Serve it over a bed of warm rice, and enjoy!

1. Combine the soy sauce, brown sugar, sriracha, sesame oil, garlic, and ginger in a small bowl.

2. Whisk together the water and cornstarch in another small bowl to make a slurry until there are no lumps. Add to the bowl with the sauce.

3. Heat the canola oil in a medium saucepan over medium-high heat. Add the beef pieces, and lightly fry until they begin to brown, about 3 minutes.

4. Reduce the heat to low. When the pan has cooled down some, after about 5 minutes, add the sauce. Simmer until the sauce thickens and absorbs evenly into the beef pieces, 3 to 5 minutes.

5. Serve over a bed of warm rice, garnish with lots of scallions and sesame seeds, and drizzle with sriracha.

2 tablespoons soy sauce
1½ tablespoons brown sugar
1 tablespoon sriracha
2 teaspoons sesame oil
1 teaspoon minced garlic
1 teaspoon minced ginger
¼ cup water
2 teaspoons cornstarch
1 tablespoon canola oil
¼ batch Beef (page 28), torn into bite-size pieces

for serving
Cooked rice
Chopped scallions
Sesame seeds
Sriracha

note
If you're preparing only a quarter of a batch of the Beef for this recipe, reduce the steaming time to 30 to 35 minutes, until firm.

takeout 135

chimichangas

makes 2 chimichangas

Jackfruit makes a delicious meat substitute in a variety of dishes, but I find that it works especially well in Mexican food! Jackfruit's fairly neutral, slightly sweet flavor makes it a fantastic base because it fully absorbs the flavors of the seasonings it's cooked in. Here, we're loading up the jackfruit with tons of spices, onions, fire-roasted chiles, and fresh lime juice to create the perfect bite.

1. Rinse and drain the jackfruit, and pat it dry with a paper towel. Gently pull apart the pieces to give the jackfruit a shredded appearance.

2. Combine the garlic powder, onion powder, chili powder, salt, coriander, cumin, paprika, and pepper in a large bowl. Add the jackfruit, and toss to coat.

3. Heat the olive oil in a medium skillet over medium heat. Add the onion, and sauté until translucent, 1 to 2 minutes.

4. Add the jackfruit, green chiles, lime juice, and vinegar, and sauté until the jackfruit starts to crisp, about 5 minutes.

5. Place half of the Monterey Jack in the center of each tortilla. Place half of the jackfruit mixture on top of the cheese, and wrap into a burrito.

6. Heat another medium skillet over medium heat, and add 1 inch of canola oil. Add the chimichangas, and fry until crispy and golden brown, about 8 minutes.

7. Serve with sour cream, pico de gallo, hot sauce, and lime wedges.

One 10-ounce can young green jackfruit
1 teaspoon garlic powder
1 teaspoon onion powder
1 teaspoon chili powder
1 teaspoon salt
½ teaspoon ground coriander
½ teaspoon ground cumin
¼ teaspoon smoked paprika
Black pepper, to taste
2 tablespoons olive oil
½ small yellow onion, finely chopped
2 tablespoons canned fire-roasted green chiles
1 tablespoon lime juice
1 teaspoon apple cider vinegar
½ cup shredded Monterey Jack
2 large flour tortillas
Canola oil, for frying

for serving
Sour cream
Pico de gallo
Hot sauce (I like El Yucateco Black Label Reserve)
Lime wedges

chicken fried rice

serves 2

No other takeout hits quite the same as the classic chicken fried rice. You can pair this dish with Orange Chicken (page 131) or Teriyaki Chicken (page 128), or simply drizzle it with some sriracha and enjoy it on its own!

1 tablespoon canola oil
1 egg
¼ cup frozen vegetables (I recommend carrots, peas, and corn)
¼ batch Chicken 2.0 (page 21), torn into bite-size pieces
1½ cups cooked long-grain rice
1 tablespoon soy sauce
2 teaspoons sriracha, or to taste
1 teaspoon rice vinegar
Salt and black pepper, to taste

for serving
Chopped scallions
Chili oil
Sriracha

1. Heat the canola oil in a medium skillet over medium-high heat. Add the egg, and stir-fry for about 1 minute.

2. Add the frozen vegetables, and stir-fry for 2 to 3 minutes. The veggies should remain crisp and bright.

3. Add the chicken, and stir-fry until crisp and brown, 2 to 3 minutes.

4. Add the rice, soy sauce, sriracha, vinegar, salt, and pepper. Continue to stir-fry until the sauces are absorbed into the rice, 2 to 3 minutes.

5. Top with scallions, chili oil, and sriracha, and serve.

note
If you're preparing only a quarter of a batch of the Chicken 2.0 for this recipe, reduce the steaming time to 35 to 40 minutes.

takeout 139

sofritas

serves 4

"Tofu tastes like nothing" is typically thrown around as an insult, but in reality, this is one of tofu's many superpowers as a base ingredient in dishes. Its spongy texture thoroughly and evenly absorbs the flavors of whatever you coat it in. That's why an extra-firm tofu block is perfect for this recipe's marinade: The flavors seep through into each and every bite.

1. Preheat an air fryer to 400°F.

2. Place the tofu in the air fryer for 30 minutes, until the tofu is lightly golden brown. Remove from the air fryer and let cool at room temperature for 5 to 10 minutes.

3. Crumble the tofu and then return it to the 400°F air fryer for another 10 to 12 minutes, until the edges start to turn golden brown.

4. Heat the olive oil in a large skillet over medium heat. Add the onion, and sauté until translucent, about 1 minute. Add the garlic, and sauté for 30 seconds.

5. Reduce the heat to low. Add the chili powder, chipotle powder, cumin, and oregano. Mix well, and sauté for 30 seconds.

6. Add the tomato paste, and cook until the oil starts separating slightly from the tomato sauce, another 2 to 3 minutes. Add a splash of water if needed to help the tomato paste separate.

7. Add the water, bay leaves, bouillon paste, vinegar, salt, and pepper. Add the tofu, and stir. Cover the skillet with a lid, and simmer, stirring periodically to prevent the mixture from burning, until the liquid reduces by about three quarters, 20 to 30 minutes.

8. Serve the sofritas in tortillas with hot sauce and salsa.

One 16-ounce package extra-firm tofu, drained and pressed
3 tablespoons olive oil
½ medium yellow onion, chopped
3 tablespoons chopped garlic
1 teaspoon chili powder
1 teaspoon chipotle powder
1 teaspoon ground cumin
½ teaspoon dried Mexican oregano
3 tablespoons tomato paste
2½ cups water
4 small bay leaves
1 teaspoon vegetable bouillon paste
1 teaspoon white wine vinegar
Salt and black pepper, to taste

for serving
Tortillas
Hot sauce
Salsa

make it meatless

spicy wontons

makes 20 to 25 wontons

These mouthwatering meat and veggie wontons are covered in a bold, aromatic, spicy Sichuan sauce. We're using textured vegetable protein (TVP) in the Meat Crumbles (page 33) to create the perfect minced meat texture in every bite.

1. Heat the canola oil in a large skillet over medium heat. Add the shallot, and sauté until translucent, about 1 minute. Add the garlic and ginger, and sauté until fragrant, 1 more minute.

2. Add the cabbage, soy sauce, salt, and pepper, and sauté until the cabbage wilts completely and reduces in volume, about 5 minutes.

3. Add the meat crumbles, and sauté until lightly crispy, 3 to 5 minutes. Let cool.

4. **Make the sauce:** Mix the soy sauce, vinegar, sesame oil, brown sugar, chili oil, garlic, Sichuan peppercorns, red pepper flakes, Chinese five spice, and salt in a small bowl.

5. Place the scallions in a separate small, heat-safe bowl.

6. Heat a small skillet over medium heat, add the sauce mixture, and simmer until fragrant, 1 to 2 minutes. Remove the sauce from the heat, immediately pour it over the scallions, and stir to combine.

7. Fill another small bowl with water. Dip your index fingertip into the water and gently wet the edges of a wonton wrapper. Add about 1 tablespoon of the filling to the center of the wrapper and fold the wrapper diagonally in half to form a triangle shape. Fold the bottom two corners of the triangle inward together to the center, and press firmly to stick. You can add a little dab of water with your fingertip if needed. Repeat with the remaining wrappers and filling.

8. Set up a bamboo steamer basket: Select a pot wide enough for the steamer basket to rest inside without touching the water at the bottom. Fill the pot with 1 to 2 inches of water. (The basket should not be submerged in the water.) Line the basket with parchment paper, and place about eight wontons at a time on top. Cover and steam for 5 minutes.

9. Remove the wontons from the steamer basket, pour the sauce on top, and serve.

3 tablespoons canola oil
1 shallot, finely chopped
3 garlic cloves, finely chopped
1 teaspoon minced ginger
½ medium head cabbage, chopped (about 3 cups)
1 tablespoon soy sauce
Salt and black pepper, to taste
½ batch Meat Crumbles (page 33; see Note)
20 to 25 wonton wrappers

sauce
¼ cup soy sauce
1 tablespoon plus 1 teaspoon black vinegar
1 tablespoon toasted sesame oil
1 tablespoon brown sugar
1½ teaspoons chili oil
3 large garlic cloves, finely chopped
½ teaspoon Sichuan peppercorns, crushed
½ teaspoon red pepper flakes
¼ teaspoon Chinese five spice
¼ teaspoon salt
⅓ cup chopped scallions

note
When cooking the meat crumbles for this recipe, shorten the cook time by 1 to 2 minutes to prevent overcooking.

takeout

butter chicken

serves 3 to 4

With the wide variety of delicious food that India has to offer, if the only dish you've ever tried is butter chicken, I might have to give you just a *little* bit of side-eye. Just a hint. But even I can acknowledge that butter chicken has a cult following for a reason. It's just that good. As a vegetarian, I normally opt for butter paneer instead, but if you're craving that classic chicken texture, try this recipe. (You can swap in about 10 ounces of cubed paneer for the Chicken 2.0 if you'd like to try the paneer version after all.)

1. Heat the butter in a medium saucepan over medium heat. Add the onion, and sauté until translucent, about 1 minute. Add the garlic and ginger, and sauté until fragrant, 1 more minute.

2. Reduce the heat to low. Add the chile powder, cumin, garam masala, fenugreek leaves, and turmeric, and sauté until fragrant, about 1 minute.

3. Add the tomatoes, cashews, and salt. Increase the heat to medium, and sauté until the tomatoes soften, 5 to 7 minutes.

4. Add the water, stir to combine, and bring to a simmer.

5. Reduce the heat to low, cover the pan, and simmer, stirring every 5 minutes or so to ensure it doesn't burn or stick to the bottom of the pan, for 25 to 30 minutes.

6. Remove from the heat and let cool to room temperature. Blend with an immersion blender, or transfer to a high-speed blender and blend. Strain the blended mixture through a sieve to remove any excess cashew pulp.

7. Return the mixture to the saucepan, and add the half-and-half, sugar, and extra water, if needed, to achieve a gravy-like consistency.

8. Heat the canola oil in a separate medium saucepan over medium heat. Add the chicken, and sauté until golden brown and crispy, about 3 minutes. Add the chicken to the gravy.

9. Return the saucepan to medium heat, and simmer until the chicken has absorbed the gravy mixture, 10 minutes.

10. Garnish with the heavy cream and cilantro, and serve.

3 tablespoons salted butter
1 cup finely chopped yellow onion
1 tablespoon finely chopped garlic
1 tablespoon crushed ginger
1½ teaspoons Kashmiri red chile powder
1¼ teaspoons ground cumin
1 teaspoon garam masala
1 teaspoon dried fenugreek leaves
¼ teaspoon ground turmeric
1 cup canned diced tomatoes
25 cashews (1 to 1.5 ounces)
Salt, to taste
1 cup water, plus more as needed
½ cup half-and-half or evaporated milk
1 teaspoon sugar
1 tablespoon canola oil
⅓ batch Chicken 2.0 (page 21; see Note), torn into bite-size pieces

for serving
2 or 3 tablespoons heavy cream
Chopped fresh cilantro

note

If you're preparing only a third of a batch of the Chicken 2.0 for this recipe, reduce the cooking time to 40 to 45 minutes.

make it meatless

beef and broccoli

serves 2 to 3

This spin on the classic Chinese take-out dish features beefy strips covered in a sweet and savory soy-based sauce, sautéed with fresh, crisp broccoli. Serve over a warm bed of rice for the best bite.

1. **Make the sauce:** Place the brown sugar, light soy sauce, oyster sauce, dark soy sauce, sesame oil, cornstarch, vinegar, red pepper flakes, white pepper, and water in a medium bowl, and whisk until evenly combined.

2. **Make the beef and broccoli:** Heat the canola oil in a medium skillet over medium heat. Add the garlic and ginger, and sauté until fragrant, about 1 minute.

3. Add the beef and broccoli, and sauté until the broccoli is slightly tender but still bright in color, 2 minutes.

4. Add the sauce, and sauté until it thickens and evenly coats everything in the pan, 3 to 4 minutes.

5. Serve over a bed of warm rice, garnished with sesame seeds.

sauce
- ¼ cup brown sugar, firmly packed
- 2 tablespoons light soy sauce
- 2 tablespoons vegetarian oyster sauce (I like Wan Ja Shan)
- 1 tablespoon dark soy sauce
- 1 tablespoon toasted sesame oil
- 1 tablespoon cornstarch
- 2 teaspoons rice vinegar
- ½ teaspoon red pepper flakes
- ⅛ teaspoon white pepper
- ¼ cup water

beef and broccoli
- 1 tablespoon canola oil
- 3 garlic cloves, finely chopped
- ¾ inch ginger, finely chopped
- ½ batch Beef (page 28; see Note), cut into thick strips
- 1 small head broccoli, cut into florets

for serving
Cooked rice
Sesame seeds

note

If you're preparing only half of a batch of the Beef for this recipe, reduce the steaming time to 35 to 40 minutes.

takeout

fried
chick

en

These fried chicken recipes are so good, they needed their own chapter.

chicken nuggets

serves 2

Before I became vegetarian, I was obsessed with a certain popular fast-food chain whose brand ambassador is literally a guy in a clown suit. Anyway, it makes really good chicken nuggets. But these might be better. We're using The Best Frozen Tofu Technique (page 39) to create a perfect meat-like texture that's just as good as fast food.

1. For the best flavor, prepare the tofu using The Best Frozen Tofu Technique (page 39). Otherwise, drain the tofu, wrap in paper towels, and press under a heavy pot or pan for 15 minutes to remove the excess water.

2. Cut the slab of tofu into small oval pieces about 2 inches long, 1½ inches wide, and ½ inch thick.

3. Create a batter station. **Make the wet batter:** Whisk together the flour, chile powder, garlic powder, onion powder, salt, and water in a medium shallow bowl until no lumps remain.

4. **Make the dry batter:** Mix together the flour, panko breadcrumbs, chile powder, garlic powder, onion powder, and salt in another medium shallow bowl.

5. Dip each piece of tofu in the wet batter to evenly coat, and let the excess drip off. Place each piece of tofu in the dry batter, and coat evenly on both sides. Gently press the dry batter into the tofu so it adheres well.

6. Heat 2 inches of oil in a heavy, medium skillet over medium heat.

7. Divide the nuggets into two batches. Gently place the first batch in the oil, and cook until crispy and golden brown, about 5 minutes. Transfer the cooked nuggets to a plate, and repeat with the second batch.

8. Serve with honey mustard and ranch dressing.

One 16-ounce block extra-firm tofu
Neutral oil (such as vegetable or canola), for frying

wet batter
1 cup all-purpose flour
1 teaspoon Kashmiri red chile powder
1 teaspoon garlic powder
1 teaspoon onion powder
1 teaspoon salt
1¼ cups water

dry batter
1 cup all-purpose flour
1 cup Japanese-style panko breadcrumbs
1 teaspoon Kashmiri red chile powder
1 teaspoon garlic powder
1 teaspoon onion powder
1 teaspoon salt

for serving
Honey mustard
Ranch dressing

chicken parmesan

serves 2

I'm pretty sure that nonnas everywhere aren't going to be pleased that I made chicken Parm using tofu, but that's a risk I'm willing to take to bring this recipe to you. We aren't using any ordinary tofu here; we're applying The Best Frozen Tofu Technique (page 39) to give the tofu a meaty texture and flavor that's perfect for this recipe.

1 **Make the chicken:** Prepare the tofu using The Best Frozen Tofu Technique (page 39), omitting the soy sauce. Cut the tofu lengthwise into two slabs and then cut around the corners of each slab to create an oval shape. Dust each slab with 1 tablespoon of flour. (This will soak up any excess moisture and help the batter stick.)

2 **Make the marinara sauce:** Heat the olive oil in a small pot over medium heat. Add the onion, and sauté until translucent, about 1 minute. Add the garlic, and sauté until fragrant, about 30 seconds. Add the red pepper flakes, and sauté for another 30 seconds.

3 Add the crushed tomatoes and basil leaves, and mix well. Cover the pot, and reduce the heat to low. Let the sauce simmer, stirring occasionally, until thickened, about 20 minutes.

4 Create a batter station. **Make the wet batter:** Mix the flour, garlic powder, onion powder, red pepper flakes, salt, Italian seasoning, black pepper, and water in a medium shallow bowl until no lumps remain.

5 **Make the dry batter:** Mix the panko breadcrumbs, Parmesan, garlic powder, onion powder, red pepper flakes, salt, Italian seasoning, and black pepper in another medium shallow bowl.

6 Dip each tofu slab first in the wet batter and then in the dry batter. Gently press the dry batter into the tofu so it sticks.

7 Heat 1 inch of canola oil in a large skillet over medium heat. Gently place the tofu slabs in the skillet, and fry, flipping every minute or so, until golden brown, about 5 minutes total.

8 If using an oven, preheat the broiler. Line a small baking sheet with foil. If using an air fryer, line the basket with foil. Place the chicken on the foil, and cover it with the marinara. Divide the Parmesan and mozzarella between the chicken pieces.

9 Broil or air-fry for 3 minutes, or until the cheese melts and starts to brown. Serve.

One 14-ounce package extra-firm tofu
2 tablespoons all-purpose flour
Canola oil, for frying
¼ cup freshly grated Parmesan
¼ cup freshly grated mozzarella

marinara sauce
¼ cup olive oil
1 small yellow onion, chopped
8 garlic cloves, chopped
½ teaspoon red pepper flakes
One 28-ounce can crushed tomatoes
6 large fresh basil leaves, torn

wet batter
½ cup all-purpose flour
½ teaspoon garlic powder
½ teaspoon onion powder
½ teaspoon red pepper flakes
½ teaspoon salt
¼ teaspoon Italian seasoning
Black pepper, to taste
½ cup plus 2 tablespoons water

dry batter
½ cup Japanese-style panko breadcrumbs
¼ cup grated Parmesan
½ teaspoon garlic powder
½ teaspoon onion powder
½ teaspoon red pepper flakes
½ teaspoon salt
¼ teaspoon Italian seasoning
Black pepper, to taste

fried chicken

enoki mushroom fried chicken

serves 2

The long, stringy fibers in enoki mushrooms perfectly recreate the juicy texture of fried chicken in this recipe. We'll cover our shrooms with a delicious seasoned batter and fry them to golden perfection. The result? A satisfying, crunchy exterior with a succulent, pull-apart interior that looks just like the real thing.

5.3 ounces enoki mushrooms
½ cup all-purpose flour
1 tablespoon cornstarch
¾ teaspoon onion powder
¾ teaspoon garlic powder
¾ teaspoon Kashmiri red chile powder
¾ teaspoon salt
¼ teaspoon smoked paprika
½ cup plus 2 tablespoons water
Canola oil, for frying

sauce
¼ cup mayonnaise
1 tablespoon gochujang paste

1. Cut off the ends of the mushrooms. Rinse the mushrooms in cold water, and pat dry with a paper towel.

2. Whisk together the flour, cornstarch, onion powder, garlic powder, chile powder, salt, and paprika in a small bowl. Add the water, and whisk again until the consistency is similar to pancake batter.

3. Heat 2 inches of oil in a medium skillet over medium heat.

4. Pull apart the mushrooms, place them in the batter, and toss until they are evenly coated. Divide the mushrooms into four portions, and gently clump each portion together to form the chicken pieces.

5. Gently place the mushrooms in the skillet, and fry, turning every minute or so, until golden brown and crispy, 5 to 6 minutes total. Transfer to a paper towel–lined plate to drain.

6. **Make the sauce:** Mix the mayonnaise and gochujang in a small bowl.

7. Serve the fried chicken with the sauce on the side.

make it meatless

nashville hot chicken tenders

serves 1 to 2

Who isn't a sucker for Southern charm and (more importantly) Southern cooking? These ultra-crispy deep-fried chicken tenders pack a punch but finish off sweet. How fitting.

1. Create a batter station. **Make the dry batter:** Mix the panko breadcrumbs, flour, salt, garlic powder, onion powder, chile powder, and paprika in a medium shallow bowl.

2. **Make the wet batter:** Mix the flour, garlic powder, onion powder, chile powder, paprika, water, hot sauce, and pickle juice in another medium shallow bowl until no lumps remain.

3. Break apart the oyster mushrooms, and clump them together, shaping them to form chicken tenders.

4. Generously coat the mushroom pieces in the wet batter, letting any excess batter drip off. Transfer the mushroom pieces to the dry batter, and gently toss to coat evenly.

5. Gently press more of the dry batter, 2 to 3 tablespoons at a time, into the wet battered mushroom pieces until the mixture starts to slightly clump together. At first, the mixture will dampen. Continue until the outer layer appears dry. (You may not need to use all the dry batter.)

6. Heat the oil to about 350°F in a large skillet over medium heat. Gently place the mushroom pieces into the oil. Do not flip the mushrooms or move them around the pan for 1 minute; this will ensure the batter won't fall off. Cook the mushrooms until crispy and golden brown, 3 to 5 minutes. Remove the mushrooms from the oil, and transfer to a paper towel–lined plate to drain.

7. **Make the sauce:** Combine the honey, brown sugar, cayenne, chili powder, hot sauce, garlic powder, onion powder, salt, and paprika in a small bowl. Slowly add ¾ cup of the hot frying oil, a little at a time, whisking continuously to combine.

8. Gently dip the tenders into the sauce until evenly coated. Serve.

chicken
- 6 ounces oyster mushrooms
- 2 cups vegetable oil

dry batter
- 1 cup Japanese-style panko breadcrumbs
- ½ cup all-purpose flour
- 1 tablespoon salt
- 1 teaspoon garlic powder
- 1 teaspoon onion powder
- 1 teaspoon Kashmiri red chile powder
- ½ teaspoon smoked paprika

wet batter
- ½ cup all-purpose flour
- 1 teaspoon garlic powder
- 1 teaspoon onion powder
- 1 teaspoon Kashmiri red chile powder
- ½ teaspoon smoked paprika
- ¾ cup water
- 2 tablespoons Louisiana hot sauce
- 2 tablespoons pickle juice

sauce
- 2 tablespoons honey
- 2 tablespoons brown sugar
- 1 tablespoon cayenne
- 1 tablespoon chili powder
- 1 tablespoon Louisiana hot sauce
- 1 teaspoon garlic powder
- 1 teaspoon onion powder
- 1 teaspoon salt
- ½ teaspoon smoked paprika

fried chicken

hot honey chicken rolls

serves 4

These hot honey chicken rolls have everything you want in a fried chicken sandwich. Warm French rolls are stuffed with crispy, golden-brown oyster mushroom chicken that's been drenched in a sweet and spicy hot honey sauce and topped with a tangy coleslaw.

1 batch Nashville Hot Chicken Tenders (page 159), prepared through step 5
½ to 1 batch Hot Honey (page 248; see Note)
4 French rolls, toasted
Pickles, optional

coleslaw
¼ cup mayonnaise
1 tablespoon olive oil
2 teaspoons coarse-ground Dijon mustard
2 teaspoons white wine vinegar
1 teaspoon honey
Salt and black pepper, to taste
8.5 ounces shredded cabbage and carrots

1. Evenly coat the chicken tenders in the hot honey using a basting brush. (Or dip the chicken tenders directly into the hot honey.) Set aside.

2. **Make the coleslaw:** Whisk together the mayonnaise, oil, mustard, vinegar, honey, salt, and pepper in a medium bowl.

3. Add the cabbage and carrots, and toss to coat.

4. Pack the rolls with the hot honey tenders, coleslaw, and pickles, if using. Serve.

note

For a saucier hot honey roll, make a full batch of the hot honey. Store any leftover sauce in an airtight container at room temperature for up to 1 week.

160   make it meatless

chicken and waffles

serves 2

This dish features crispy fried chicken with spicy maple syrup on a homemade waffle. (Or a store-bought one if you want. I'm not here to judge). This savory and sweet powerhouse meal is perfect for breakfast, lunch, brunch, and honestly, even dinner.

1 Mix the flour, sugar, baking powder, baking soda, and salt in a small bowl.

2 Beat the egg in a medium bowl. Whisk in the milk, butter, and vanilla extract.

3 Add the dry ingredients to the wet ingredients, and mix until the batter is smooth and no lumps remain. Add more milk, 1 tablespoon at a time, as needed to loosen the texture of the batter. It should be thick but spreadable.

4 Preheat a waffle maker, and grease it with about 2 teaspoons oil or butter. Using about ¼ cup of the batter for each waffle, cook the waffles until they turn a deep golden brown, 4 to 6 minutes.

5 **Make the syrup:** Mix the maple syrup, butter, and hot sauce in a small bowl.

6 Add a piece of fried chicken on top of each waffle, drizzle generously with the syrup, and serve.

1 cup all-purpose flour
¼ cup sugar
½ teaspoon baking powder
½ teaspoon baking soda
¼ teaspoon salt
1 egg
½ cup milk, plus more as needed
1 tablespoon salted butter, melted
½ teaspoon bourbon vanilla extract
Canola oil or salted butter, for greasing
1 batch Classic Fried Chicken (page 27)

syrup
¾ cup maple syrup
3 tablespoons salted butter, melted
3 tablespoons Louisiana hot sauce

fried chicken

karaage

makes 2 large wings

This crispy Japanese fried chicken uses my favorite meat substitute (please don't tell the others): oyster mushrooms! Nothing beats oyster mushrooms when it comes to recreating the juicy, meaty texture of fried chicken. Here, we marinate the shrooms and cover them in a classic potato starch dredge for the perfect crisp. We're making a quick sriracha mayo sauce to serve with this dish, but it also pairs well with Bang Bang Sauce (page 246).

1. Combine the soy sauce, ginger, mirin, sesame oil, garlic powder, and white pepper in a zipper bag.

2. Add the mushrooms, massage until evenly coated in the marinade, and set aside to marinate for 15 minutes.

3. Whisk together the potato starch and cornstarch in a shallow bowl.

4. Remove the mushrooms from the bag, and gently squeeze out as much excess marinade as possible. Wrap the mushrooms in a paper towel, and gently pat to remove any remaining moisture.

5. Tightly clump together and mold the mushrooms into two "wings" by pressing them firmly in the palms of your hands. Dip the wings into the starch mixture, and firmly press the mixture onto the wings to get a thick, even coating around each wing. Gently squeeze the mushrooms in your palms to clump them back into wing shapes as needed.

6. Heat 2 inches of canola oil in a small pot over medium heat. Add the wings, and fry until crispy and golden brown, 5 to 6 minutes.

7. **Make the sauce:** Mix the mayonnaise, sriracha, lemon juice, sugar, salt, and pepper in a bowl.

8. Serve the wings with the sauce on the side or drizzled on top.

---

3 tablespoons soy sauce
½ inch ginger, grated
2 teaspoons mirin
1 teaspoon toasted sesame oil
½ teaspoon garlic powder
¼ teaspoon white pepper
8 ounces oyster mushrooms
½ cup potato starch
2 tablespoons cornstarch
Canola oil, for frying

sauce

2 tablespoons Kewpie mayonnaise
1 teaspoon sriracha
½ teaspoon lemon juice
½ teaspoon sugar
Salt and black pepper, to taste

watch me make this!

make it meatless

seare
grille

d &
d

Delicious staples to slap on the grill this summer.

steak
with garlic-chive butter and asparagus
serves 2 to 4

This isn't your dad's steak recipe! We're subbing in a meaty chickpea seitan for regular steak and cooking it in a beetroot soy sauce for the perfect umami flavor. (The garlic chive butter is also great on mashed potatoes, if you were wondering.)

1 **Make the steak:** Place the chickpeas, ⅔ cup water, 2 tablespoons soy sauce, 1 tablespoon oil, 2 teaspoons beetroot powder, bouillon paste, garlic powder, liquid smoke, mustard, nutritional yeast, onion powder, cumin, paprika, and white pepper in a blender, and blend until smooth, about 1 minute.

2 Transfer the chickpea mixture to a large bowl. Add the vital wheat gluten, and mix. Turn out the mixture onto a flat surface, and knead into a tough dough, about 5 minutes.

3 Divide the dough into two large or four small portions, and mold the dough into steak shapes. The dough will be tough, so you may need to pound it down with your fist.

4 Set up a steamer basket: Place a metal steamer basket in a large pot. The steamer basket should be small enough to fit inside the pot with the lid closed. Add enough water to the pot to reach just below the steamer basket. (The basket should not be submerged in the water.) Bring the water to a boil over high heat and then reduce the heat to medium.

5 Wrap the steaks in foil, add to the steamer, cover, and steam for 45 minutes. Make sure to top up the pot with water as needed. There should always be at least 1 inch water in the bottom of the pot.

6 Use tongs to remove the steaks from the steamer, and unwrap immediately.

steak
- 1 cup rinsed and drained canned chickpeas
- 1½ cups plus ⅔ cup water, divided
- 4 tablespoons soy sauce, divided
- 3 tablespoons olive oil, divided
- 2 tablespoons plus 2 teaspoons beetroot powder, divided
- 2 teaspoons vegetable bouillon paste
- 1 teaspoon garlic powder
- 1 teaspoon liquid smoke
- 1 teaspoon stone-ground mustard
- 1 teaspoon nutritional yeast
- 1 teaspoon onion powder
- ¼ teaspoon ground cumin
- ¼ teaspoon smoked paprika
- ⅛ teaspoon white pepper
- 2 cups vital wheat gluten (I recommend Anthony's)

garlic chive butter
- 10 tablespoons salted butter, at room temperature
- 3 garlic cloves, grated
- 1 tablespoon chopped fresh chives
- 1 teaspoon chipotle powder
- Juice of ½ lime
- Himalayan salt and black pepper, to taste

asparagus
- One 16-ounce bunch asparagus
- 1 tablespoon extra virgin olive oil
- Sea salt and black pepper, to taste
- 1 lemon wedge

make it meatless

7 Heat the remaining 2 tablespoons oil in a medium pan over medium heat. Add the steaks, and sear for about 2 minutes per side.

8 Mix 1½ cups water, the remaining 2 tablespoons soy sauce, and 2 tablespoons beetroot powder in a small bowl. Pour this liquid over the steak in the skillet, and cook, flipping the steak often, until most of the liquid is absorbed and the remaining liquid is thick and bubbling, about 5 minutes.

9 **Make the butter:** Combine the butter, garlic, chives, chipotle powder, lime juice, Himalayan salt, and pepper in a small bowl.

10 **Make the asparaus:** Set up the steamer basket again. Add the asparagus, cover, and steam until the asparagus is softened but remains bright green, 3 to 4 minutes.

11 Remove from the steamer, and transfer to a serving plate. Top with the olive oil, sea salt, pepper, and a squeeze of lemon juice.

12 Slice the steak into ¼-inch-thick pieces. You can pour the remaining liquid on top of the steak after you've sliced it. Serve the steak on top of the asparagus with the garlic chive butter on top.

seared & grilled

steak
with chimichurri

serves 1

Lion's mane mushrooms offer myriad health benefits, but their other superpower is their satisfying meaty texture. They're not cheap (just like a fine cut of regular steak) but are worth the splurge for when that red meat craving really hits. And everyone knows that the best way to eat steak is with a generous drizzle of chimichurri sauce (duh).

1. Whisk together the soy sauce, olive oil, beetroot powder, bouillon paste, garlic powder, onion powder, liquid smoke, maple syrup, miso paste, paprika, and apple cider vinegar in a large bowl.

2. Add the mushrooms, massage until evenly coated, and set aside to marinate for about 10 minutes.

3. Heat the canola oil in a medium skillet over medium heat.

4. Gently wrap the mushrooms in paper towels to soak up the excess marinade. Using tongs, place the mushrooms in the pan, and press them down gently. Flip the mushrooms, and press again to coat both sides evenly in the oil. Place a heavy bowl or plate on top of the mushrooms in the skillet, and press down firmly with your hands. Cook, keeping the pressure applied, until the mushrooms start to compress, 1 to 2 minutes.

5. Flip over the mushrooms and repeat, applying pressure until the mushrooms compress further, 1 to 2 minutes. Continue flipping and pressing until the mushrooms flatten out and are even in shape, 3 to 4 minutes total. Use caution while doing this: Moisture released from the mushrooms may splatter.

6. Set aside the heavy bowl or plate and continue searing the mushrooms, pressing with a spatula and flipping every 1 or 2 minutes as needed, until they are deep golden brown and have released all of their moisture, 7 or 8 minutes total. For more pressure, you can use your tongs to press down on the spatula. Remove the skillet from the heat.

7. **Make the chimichurri:** Place the parsley, olive oil, red wine vinegar, garlic, shallot, chile, lime juice, oregano, salt, if using, and pepper in a small blender, and pulse until evenly chopped but not pureed. (You can also grind the ingredients in a molcajete.)

8. Drizzle a generous helping of the chimichurri over the steak, or on the side, and serve.

- 2 tablespoons dark soy sauce
- 1 tablespoon olive oil
- 2 teaspoons beetroot powder
- ¾ teaspoon vegetable bouillon paste
- ½ teaspoon garlic powder
- ½ teaspoon onion powder
- ½ teaspoon liquid smoke
- ½ teaspoon maple syrup
- ½ teaspoon red miso paste
- ¼ teaspoon smoked paprika
- ⅛ teaspoon apple cider vinegar
- 8 ounces lion's mane mushrooms
- 1 tablespoon canola oil

chimichurri
- 1 bunch fresh Italian parsley
- ¼ cup extra virgin olive oil
- 2 to 3 tablespoons red wine vinegar
- 3 large garlic cloves
- ¼ shallot
- 1 Fresno chile
- 1 teaspoon lime juice
- 1 teaspoon dried oregano
- Salt, to taste, optional (see Note)
- Black pepper, to taste

note
The steak is salt-forward, so you may want to skip adding salt to the chimichurri for balance.

watch me make this!

seared & grilled

tandoori chicken rolls

makes 2 rolls

These stunning tandoori chicken rolls encompass all the things I love about Indian street food: They're bright, vibrant, and absolutely bursting with flavor. We marinate meaty oyster mushrooms in a classic tandoori yogurt marinade, char them in the oven, top them off with a delicious earthy green chutney, and throw it all into a soft naan.

1. Preheat the oven to 400°F. Line a baking sheet with parchment paper.

2. Combine the yogurt, fenugreek, oil, lemon juice, chile powder, coriander, garlic, ginger, salt, garam masala, turmeric, and food coloring in a medium bowl.

3. Add the mushrooms and massage well with your hands until the mushrooms slightly soften and are coated with the marinade. Set aside to marinate for about 15 minutes.

4. Transfer the mushrooms to the prepared baking sheet, and clump them into a loaf shape in the center of the tray. Bake for 35 to 40 minutes, flipping halfway through, until crispy and slightly charred. It's okay if the loaf falls apart.

5. Heat a medium skillet over medium-high heat. Add the mushrooms, and sear for a deeper char, 3 to 5 minutes.

6. Heat the naans according to the package instructions.

7. Add half of the tandoori chicken to the center of each naan, and drizzle with some of the green chutney. Squeeze the lemon wedges over the top, add the red onions, and serve.

½ cup Greek yogurt (see Note)
1½ tablespoons fenugreek leaves
1½ tablespoons canola oil
2 teaspoons lemon juice
1½ teaspoons Kashmiri red chile powder
1 teaspoon ground coriander
1 teaspoon minced garlic
1 teaspoon grated fresh ginger
1 teaspoon salt
½ teaspoon garam masala
¼ teaspoon ground turmeric
10 drops red gel food coloring
8 ounces oyster mushrooms
2 naans
Green Chutney (page 247)
Lemon wedges
Finely chopped red onion

note

If you like your spice level on the milder side, add a couple extra tablespoons of Greek yogurt to the chutney to cool things down a bit.

make it meatless

gyros

serves 2

This classic Greek dish consists of a warm pita filled with perfectly spiced mushroom meat, a cool tzatziki sauce, crisp lettuce, tangy pickled onions, and fresh cherry tomatoes. We're searing the oyster mushrooms in the oven and throwing on a rich spice rub (with a little liquid smoke) to mimic the rotisserie meat normally found in gyros, and it works oh so well.

1. Combine the oil, soy sauce, garlic powder, onion powder, oregano, ponzu sauce, oyster sauce, chili powder, cumin, liquid smoke, black pepper, and dill in a medium bowl.

2. Place the mushrooms in the marinade, massage to coat them evenly, and then cover and set in the refrigerator to marinate for about 1 hour.

3. Preheat the oven to 400°F. Line a baking sheet with foil.

4. Shake off the excess marinade from the mushrooms, and transfer them to the prepared baking sheet. Bake for 20 to 25 minutes, until the edges are crispy and deep golden brown.

5. **Make the tzatziki sauce:** Grate the cucumber. Squeeze out any excess moisture.

6. Mix the yogurt, oil, lemon juice, mint, garlic, salt, and pepper in a small bowl. Add the cucumber, and mix again.

7. Heat the pitas in the oven according to the package instructions.

8. Add a generous amount (2 to 3 tablespoons) of tzatziki to the center of each pita. Top with the mushrooms, pickled onions, tomatoes, and lettuce to taste, and serve.

1½ tablespoons olive oil
1 tablespoon soy sauce
1 teaspoon garlic powder
1 teaspoon onion powder
1 teaspoon dried oregano
1 teaspoon ponzu sauce
1 teaspoon vegetarian oyster sauce (I like Wan Ja Shan)
½ teaspoon chili powder
½ teaspoon ground cumin
½ teaspoon liquid smoke
Ground black pepper, to taste
3 fresh dill sprigs
6 ounces oyster mushrooms
2 medium pitas

tzatziki
¼ large English cucumber
½ cup 5% Greek yogurt
2½ teaspoons olive oil
2½ teaspoons lemon juice
3 to 5 fresh mint leaves, julienned
1 large garlic clove, minced
Salt and black pepper, to taste

for serving
Pickled red onions (see page 56)
Halved cherry tomatoes
Shredded lettuce (iceberg or romaine)

seared & grilled 175

"sea"

food

In the immortal words of Bruce, the great white shark: "Fish are friends, not food."

blackened fish

serves 2

This bold Cajun blackened fish has all the robust flavors of the sea without the seafood. The delicate layers of the banana blossoms provide the perfect fishy texture to curb those seafood cravings for good.

1. Place the fishy marinade in a large bowl.

2. Drain the banana blossoms, wrap them in a paper towel, and gently squeeze out the excess moisture. Transfer the banana blossoms to the large bowl, and massage them with the marinade until evenly distributed. Submerge the banana blossoms in the marinade, and set in the refrigerator to marinate for 1 hour.

3. Preheat an air fryer to 400°F (see Note). Remove the banana blossoms from the marinade, and squeeze out as much excess moisture as possible.

4. Divide the banana blossom mixture into two equal portions. Add ½ tablespoon of tapioca starch to each portion, and mix and squeeze until the tapioca starch dissolves, molding each portion into a filet shape. (The starch will act as a binding agent.)

5. Add ½ tablespoon of Cajun seasoning to each fillet, and rub evenly on both sides. Drizzle each fillet with 1 teaspoon oil, and gently pat in.

6. Place the fillets in an air-fryer basket and cook in the air fryer at 400°F for 20 minutes. Flip over the fillets and cook for another 5 to 7 minutes, until a crispy "skin" has formed on both sides of the banana blossom.

7. Serve the fish with a fresh squeeze of lemon juice and fries on the side.

1 batch fishy marinade (see Marinated and Battered Fish, page 36)
One 18-ounce can banana blossoms (9 ounces drained)
1 tablespoon tapioca starch
1 tablespoon Cajun seasoning
2 teaspoons olive oil

for serving
Lemon wedges
Fries

note

To prepare the fillets in the oven, preheat the oven to 425°F and place the fillets on a foil-lined baking sheet. Bake for 20 to 25 minutes, flipping halfway through, until crispy and golden brown.

crab cakes

makes 6 crab cakes

There's nothing fancier than replacing imitation crabmeat with really expensive mushrooms in these savory cakes. (Alas, I had to show you my bougie side.) When you pull apart and marinate these shrooms, they perfectly mimic the lush texture of crab cakes to a tee.

1. Break the lion's mane mushroom into small pieces and place in a medium bowl. Add the Old Bay and lemon juice, and massage with your hands until the mushrooms are evenly coated and start to soften. Set aside to marinate at room temperature until the mushrooms release their excess water, 15 minutes.

2. Wrap the mushrooms in a paper towel, and squeeze out as much excess moisture as possible. You may need to repeat this process once or twice more.

3. Discard the liquid, and dry the bottom of the bowl. Return the mushrooms to the bowl. Add the mayonnaise, celery, and mustard, and mix until combined.

4. Create a batter station. **Make the wet batter:** Combine the flour, salt, chile powder, garlic powder, onion powder, paprika, and water in a medium shallow bowl to form a pancake batter consistency. **Then make the dry batter:** Combine the panko breadcrumbs, chile powder, garlic powder, onion powder, salt, and paprika in another medium shallow bowl.

5. Form the crab cake mixture into six patties. Coat the patties in the wet batter first and let the excess drip off. Then coat them evenly in the dry batter.

6. Heat 1 inch of oil in a large skillet over medium heat. Add the patties, and cook until both sides are deep golden brown, 4 to 5 minutes per side.

7. Sprinkle with flaky sea salt and a fresh squeeze of lemon, and serve with tartar sauce.

1 large lion's mane mushroom (about 13 ounces)
1½ tablespoons Old Bay Seasoning
1½ teaspoons lemon juice
¼ cup Kewpie mayonnaise
¼ cup finely chopped celery
1 teaspoon stone-ground mustard
Canola oil, for frying

wet batter
¼ cup all-purpose flour
½ teaspoon salt
¼ teaspoon Kashmiri red chile powder
¼ teaspoon garlic powder
¼ teaspoon onion powder
⅛ teaspoon smoked paprika
¼ cup plus 2 tablespoons water

dry batter
½ cup Japanese-style panko breadcrumbs
¼ teaspoon Kashmiri red chile powder
¼ teaspoon garlic powder
¼ teaspoon onion powder
¼ teaspoon salt
⅛ teaspoon smoked paprika

for serving
Flaky sea salt
Lemon wedges
Tartar Sauce (page 247)

"sea"food

fish tacos

serves 4

Crispy banana blossom fish, tangy cabbage slaw, and spicy sriracha mayo make the perfect combination of salt, fat, acid, and heat in these lovely tacos.

1. Starting with step 5 of the Marinated and Battered Fish recipe, remove the banana blossoms from the refrigerator, form them into long fish-finger shapes, and batter and fry as directed in step 6.

2. **Make the slaw:** Thinly slice the cabbage using a mandoline. Coat the cabbage with lime juice, and sprinkle on the salt and pepper. Taste and adjust the seasonings as desired.

3. **Make the sauce:** Mix the mayonnaise, sriracha, lime juice, and honey in a small bowl.

4. Heat a medium pan over medium heat. Cook the tortillas for 15 seconds per side and then wrap them in a paper towel to keep them warm while you assemble the tacos.

5. Add one or two banana blossom pieces to each tortilla. Drizzle with some sauce, and add the slaw on top. Garnish with thin slices of avocado and hot sauce, if using, and serve.

2 batches Marinated and Battered Fish (page 36), prepared through step 4
8 to 10 street taco flour tortillas

slaw
¼ head red cabbage
Juice of 1 lime
½ teaspoon salt
½ teaspoon black pepper

sauce
2 tablespoons mayonnaise
1½ tablespoons sriracha
2 teaspoons lime juice
1 teaspoon honey

for serving, optional
Thinly sliced avocado
Hot sauce

fish and chips

serves 2

I never thought fish would become one of my favorite comfort foods. And I was right, because this fish is made with banana blossom. So ha! But for all you banana blossom nonbelievers, let me tell you, this recipe will give you all the seafood flavor goodness without any of that unmistakable *aroma* that comes with actual fish. So basically, it's the best of both worlds. Cue the *Hannah Montana* music.

2 medium russet potatoes
1 tablespoon neutral oil (such as canola or vegetable)
Salt, to taste
1 batch Marinated and Battered Fish (page 36)

for serving
Sea salt, to taste
Tartar Sauce (page 247)

1 Preheat an air fryer to 400°F.

2 Peel and cut the potatoes into thin sticks. Coat the potatoes with the oil, and season lightly with salt.

3 Separate the potatoes into two batches. Place each batch in the air fryer for 12 to 17 minutes, until golden brown. Shake the air-fryer basket halfway through the cook time to ensure even cooking.

4 Sprinkle the fries with sea salt, and serve with the fried fish and tartar sauce on the side.

crab rangoon

makes about 25 rangoons

No crustaceans were harmed in the making of this recipe. The only thing harmed was my New Year's resolution after I pounded four servings of these by myself. (And I'd do it again.) These crispy deep-fried wontons are stuffed with a rich cream cheese, king oyster mushroom, and scallion filling and served alongside a mouthwatering sweet chili sauce. Totally worth it.

1 cup whipped cream cheese
1 tablespoon soy sauce
1 teaspoon garlic powder
1 teaspoon rice vinegar
½ teaspoon salt
½ teaspoon white pepper
1 king oyster mushroom (5 to 7 ounces)
2 tablespoons finely chopped scallion
25 wonton wrappers
Canola oil, for frying
½ batch Thai Sweet Chili Sauce (page 246)

1. Mix the cream cheese, soy sauce, garlic powder, vinegar, salt, and white pepper in a large bowl.

2. Remove the cap from the king oyster mushroom. Shred the mushroom into fine long strips and then cut them into ½-inch-long pieces. (This mimics the texture of crabmeat.)

3. Fold the mushroom and scallions into the cream cheese mixture.

4. Fill a small bowl with water.

5. Add 1 tablespoon of the mixture to the center of each wonton wrapper. Dip your index fingertip into the water, and gently wet the edges of the wonton wrapper. Fold the wrapper diagonally over the filling to create a triangle shape. Gently press the edges together to close the wrapper. Repeat with the remaining filling and wrappers.

6. Heat 1 inch of oil in a medium saucepan over medium heat. Check the temperature of the oil by dipping in a chopstick; when the oil starts to lightly bubble around the chopstick, it's ready.

7. Gently place half of the crab rangoons in the oil, making sure not to overcrowd the pan. Fry until crispy and golden brown, about 2 minutes. Transfer to a paper towel–lined plate, and repeat with the second half.

8. Serve with the sweet chili sauce.

make it meatless

fried calamari

serves 3 to 4

This is crispy, beer-battered calamari—sans the beer and calamari. Instead, we're using king oyster mushrooms to recreate everyone's favorite seafood appetizer.

1. Slice the mushrooms into ½-inch discs. Using a bottle cap, punch out the center of each disc.

2. Create a batter station. **Make the wet batter:** Whisk together the egg and buttermilk in a medium bowl. **Then make the dry batter:** Mix the flour, baking soda, cornstarch, chile powder, garlic powder, onion powder, salt, pepper, and paprika in a separate medium bowl.

3. Dip each piece of mushroom into the wet mixture and then into the dry. Make sure the mushrooms are evenly coated, and gently shake off any excess.

4. Heat the oil to about 350°F in a large, heavy skillet over medium heat. To check if the oil is ready, add a few drops of the wet batter to the oil. The batter should start gently sizzling. If the oil starts sputtering, it is too hot.

5. Add the mushrooms to the skillet, and fry until golden brown, about 5 minutes. Make sure not to overcrowd the pan.

6. Garnish with lemon juice and a pinch of flaky salt, and serve with tartar sauce.

3 large king oyster mushrooms
1 egg
⅓ cup reduced-fat buttermilk
½ cup all-purpose flour
1 tablespoon plus 1 teaspoon baking soda
1 tablespoon cornstarch
1 teaspoon Kashmiri red chile powder
½ teaspoon garlic powder
½ teaspoon onion powder
½ teaspoon salt
½ teaspoon black pepper
⅛ teaspoon smoked paprika
3 cups neutral oil (such as canola or vegetable)

for serving
Lemon juice
Flaky salt
Tartar Sauce (page 247)

"sea" food

parmesan orzo
with brown butter scallops
serves 2

I rarely enjoy fine-dining restaurants because of the lack of vegetarian options. Like, no, I don't want to pay $50 for a baked potato with a side of butter lettuce, which is typically what you're left with when all the mains are focused on meat. If I had my own fine-dining restaurant, this dish would be one of the first I'd add to the menu. The rich and hearty Parmesan orzo is balanced perfectly with the nutty and toasty butter scallops. I think it would make most carnivores veg-believers!

orzo
- 2 tablespoons olive oil
- ½ small shallot, finely chopped
- 3 large garlic cloves, finely chopped
- ⅔ cup orzo
- 2 cups water
- 3½ teaspoons vegetable bouillon paste
- 2 teaspoons lemon juice
- ⅓ cup shaved Parmesan, tightly packed
- 2 tablespoons salted butter
- 1 to 2 tablespoons heavy whipping cream, to taste
- ½ teaspoon red pepper flakes

brown butter scallops
- 2 large king oyster mushrooms
- 4 tablespoons salted butter
- Sea salt, to taste
- Juice of ½ lemon
- Chopped fresh parsley, for garnish

1. **Make the orzo:** Heat a large, heavy saucepan over medium heat. Add the oil and shallots, and sauté until translucent, 30 to 60 seconds. Add the garlic, and sauté for 30 seconds.

2. Add the orzo, and toast until lightly browned, 1 to 2 minutes.

3. Mix the water and bouillon paste in a small bowl to create a veggie broth. Add the broth to the saucepan along with the lemon juice. Simmer until almost all the broth has been absorbed by the orzo, about 10 minutes. You can add ½ cup more water, if needed, to ensure the orzo is tender and cooked al dente.

4. Turn off the heat. Stir in the Parmesan, butter, heavy cream, and red pepper flakes.

5. **Make the scallops:** Slice the mushrooms into 1-inch-thick pieces.

6. Heat a small skillet over medium heat. Add the butter, and melt until the solids separate from the oil and the butter is browned and smells nutty, about 5 minutes.

7. Sprinkle the mushroom slices with salt and then add them to the skillet. Sear until the edges are deep golden brown, 3 to 5 minutes per side.

8. Turn off the heat. Add the lemon juice, and garnish with parsley.

9. Place the orzo on a large plate, place the scallops on top, and serve.

pig o

out

These little piggies did *not* go into your BLT!

sausage flatbread
with truffle pesto
serves 1

If you wanna bring a dish to a party that lets everyone know you're better than them, this is it. Everything from the homemade pesto to the truffle oil screams effortless yet luxe, light yet decadent, rich yet approachable. Just like you.

1 Preheat an air fryer to 350°F.

2 Evenly sprinkle the mozzarella, Parmesan, sausage, and sun-dried tomatoes over the flatbread.

3 Cook the flatbread in the air fryer for 5 to 8 minutes, until the cheese has fully melted, the edges of the flatbread are golden brown, and the sausage is crispy and browned.

4 Drizzle the flatbread with the pesto, red pepper flakes, more Parmesan, and truffle oil, and serve.

- ½ cup shredded mozzarella
- ¼ cup freshly grated Parmesan, plus more for serving
- 1 Sausage (page 31), broken into crumbles
- 4 sun-dried tomatoes, chopped
- 1 flatbread or naan
- Cashew Truffle Oil Pesto (page 249)
- Red pepper flakes, to taste
- ½ teaspoon white truffle oil

blt

serves 1

Bacon. Lettuce. Tomatoes. But the bacon is actually a mushroom we squeeze the living hell out of to make the texture nice and meaty. I know the shape isn't really giving bacon, but I promise the flavor is there.

1. Whisk together the mayonnaise, adobo sauce, honey, mustard, and salt in a small bowl.

2. Toast the bread until golden brown. Spread a generous amount of the sauce on one side of both slices of bread.

3. Add the tomato, lettuce, and bacon on the sauced side of one slice of bread and then top with the other slice.

4. Cut diagonally (or lengthwise, if you love chaos), and serve with a large dill pickle on the side. Store any leftover sauce in an airtight container in the refrigerator for up to 3 days.

¼ cup mayonnaise
2 teaspoons adobo sauce from canned chipotles in adobo sauce
1 teaspoon honey
¼ teaspoon Dijon mustard
Pinch of salt
2 slices sourdough, or bread of choice
2 large heirloom tomato slices
2 romaine lettuce leaves
1 batch Bacon (page 38)
1 large dill pickle

pig out 201

pad kra pao
serves 5

Need minced pork without the pork? Textured vegetable protein (TVP) to the rescue! When it's seasoned and prepared the right way, TVP creates the perfect porky meat crumble so you can make the aromatic Thai basil pork you've always dreamed of.

1. Mix the 2 cups hot water, bouillon paste, vinegar, ½ teaspoon liquid smoke, garlic powder, onion powder, paprika, and white pepper in a large bowl.

2. Add the TVP and ¼ teaspoon liquid smoke, and mix until evenly combined. Let the mixture sit until the TVP rehydrates and expands, about 5 minutes.

3. Sprinkle in the vital wheat gluten, and gently toss with your hands until the TVP is evenly coated.

4. Place the garlic and chiles in a blender, and pulse until finely ground. Transfer to a small bowl. Add the vegetable broth, oyster sauce, light soy sauce, dark soy sauce, sugar, lime juice, and black pepper, and stir to combine.

5. Heat the oil in a large skillet over medium heat. Add the TVP pork, and sauté until crispy and golden brown, about 5 minutes.

6. Add the soy sauce mixture, and sauté until the liquid is fully absorbed and the TVP pork crisps up again, 8 to 10 minutes.

7. Add the basil leaves, and sauté until fragrant, 2 to 3 minutes.

8. **Make the prik nam pla sauce:** Combine the chiles, shallot, garlic, lime juice, soy sauce, and sugar in a small bowl.

9. Soak the dried seaweed in ¼ cup hot water in a separate small bowl for 10 minutes. Squeeze the rehydrated seaweed so the flavor comes out and infuses the water, and remove and discard the seaweed.

10. Add 2 tablespoons of the seaweed water to the prik nam pla sauce, and mix well.

11. Serve the pad kra pao over a bed of warm rice with a sunny-side-up egg on top and the prik nam pla sauce on the side.

---

2 cups hot water
2 teaspoons vegetable bouillon paste
½ teaspoon apple cider vinegar
½ teaspoon plus ¼ teaspoon liquid smoke, divided
½ teaspoon garlic powder
½ teaspoon onion powder
¼ teaspoon smoked paprika
¼ teaspoon white pepper
1½ cups textured vegetable protein (TVP)
½ cup vital wheat gluten (I recommend Anthony's)
5 garlic cloves
4 Thai red chiles
¼ cup vegetable broth
3 tablespoons vegetarian oyster sauce (I like Wan Ja Shan)
3 tablespoons light soy sauce
2 tablespoons dark soy sauce
1 tablespoon sugar
Juice of ½ lime
Black pepper, to taste
⅓ cup canola oil
0.5 ounce Thai basil leaves

prik nam pla sauce
10 Thai red chiles, finely chopped
¼ shallot, finely chopped
2 large garlic cloves, finely chopped
Juice of 1 lime
2 tablespoons light soy sauce
¼ teaspoon sugar
Handful of dried seaweed
¼ cup hot water

for serving
Cooked rice
Fried sunny-side-up eggs

sausage and peppers

serves 2

This hearty dish is a flavor-packed Italian American classic. Golden-browned sausage medallions are paired with bell peppers, sweet onions, and a tangy tomato sauce that's infused with garlic and Italian herbs. Pair it with a fresh loaf of toasty bread or even a creamy pasta!

3 tablespoons olive oil
1 batch Sausage (page 31), sliced into ½-inch rounds
1 green bell pepper, sliced
1 red bell pepper, sliced
½ medium sweet onion, sliced
2 tablespoons water
1 teaspoon vegetable bouillon paste
¼ cup canned diced tomatoes
2 tablespoons tomato paste
Salt and black pepper, to taste
7 large garlic cloves, finely chopped
1 teaspoon Italian seasoning
1 teaspoon red pepper flakes
Chopped fresh parsley

1. Heat the oil in a large skillet over medium heat. Add the sausage, and cook until slightly charred, 2 to 3 minutes per side. Remove the sausage from the skillet.

2. Increase the heat to high. Add the bell peppers and onion, and sauté until the onion is slightly translucent and the peppers remain bright and crisp, about 3 minutes.

3. Mix the water and bouillon paste in a small bowl.

4. Reduce the heat to medium. Add the bouillon mixture, tomatoes, tomato paste, salt, and pepper, and cook until the tomatoes completely soften, 3 to 5 minutes.

5. Stir in the garlic, Italian seasoning, and red pepper flakes and then add the sausage rounds. Cook, stirring occasionally, until everything is well combined, 2 to 3 minutes.

6. Garnish with parsley, and serve.

pig out

pork buns

makes 4 buns

These soft, fluffy buns are stuffed with Chinese barbecue pork and topped with fresh scallions and a sriracha mayo drizzle. They give happiness in a bite.

1. **Make the buns:** Microwave the milk in a large mug until warm but not hot, about 45 seconds. Add the sugar and yeast, and mix well. Let sit for about 10 minutes. You may see some small bubbles on the surface as the yeast activates.

2. Combine the flour, salt, and baking powder in a large bowl. Add the yeast mixture and water, and knead, using your hands or a stand mixer with a dough hook attachment on medium-low speed, until the dough is well combined and soft, about 5 minutes.

3. Cover the bowl with a kitchen towel, and let the dough rest at room temperature until light, airy, and doubled in size, 1 hour.

4. **Make the filling:** Whisk together the soy sauce, hoisin sauce, liquid smoke, olive oil, garlic powder, onion powder, salt, and paprika in a small bowl.

5. Add the king oyster mushrooms to the marinade, massage the mushrooms with the marinade until evenly coated, and let marinate for 15 minutes. Remove the mushrooms from the marinade, wrap in paper towels, and gently squeeze out the excess liquid.

6. Heat the canola oil in a medium skillet over medium heat. Add the mushrooms, and sauté until they start to crisp and brown, 5 to 8 minutes. Turn off the heat.

7. Add the char siu sauce, and mix until the sauce evenly coats the mushrooms.

8. Divide the dough into four pieces, and use a rolling pin to roll them into thin circles, about 5 inches wide and ¼ inch thick.

9. Let the filling cool to room temperature. Divide into four portions, and add one portion to the center of each piece of dough. Gather the edges of the dough around the filling, and press the dough together firmly to close. Brush the buns with canola oil.

buns
- 1¼ cups milk or oat milk
- 2 teaspoons sugar
- One 0.25-ounce packet active dry yeast
- 3 cups all-purpose flour
- 2 tablespoons salt
- 1 tablespoon baking powder
- ⅓ cup water
- Canola oil, for brushing

filling
- 1 tablespoon dark soy sauce
- 1 teaspoon hoisin sauce
- 1 teaspoon mesquite liquid smoke
- 1 teaspoon olive oil
- ½ teaspoon garlic powder
- ½ teaspoon onion powder
- ½ teaspoon salt
- ¼ teaspoon smoked paprika
- 3 king oyster mushrooms (about 12 ounces), diced
- 1 tablespoon canola oil
- ¼ cup char siu sauce

for serving
- 3 tablespoons Kewpie mayonnaise
- 3 tablespoons sriracha sauce
- ½ bunch scallions
- Toasted sesame seeds

make it meatless

10. Set up a bamboo steamer basket: Select a pot wide enough for the steamer basket to rest inside without touching the water at the bottom. Fill the pot with 1 to 2 inches of water. (The basket should not be submerged in the water.) Line the basket with parchment paper, and add the buns. Cover and steam for 12 minutes.

11. Mix the mayonnaise and sriracha in a small bowl to create a dipping sauce.

12. Thinly slice the scallions lengthwise into long strips. Soak in an ice bath until the scallions curl, about 5 minutes. Remove them from the ice bath, and gently pat dry with a paper towel.

13. Top the buns with scallion curls and sesame seeds, and serve with the sriracha mayo (or drizzle some on top of the buns).

pig out

not s
mea

Just plants being plants. Even though this book is all about meatless options that look and taste the part, I couldn't resist including some recipes that prove that veggies taste good all on their own.

mushroom risotto

serves 2 to 3

Everyone should learn how to make a classic creamy mushroom risotto at one point in their life. So I'm here to help. Certainly, this recipe is a labor of love and requires some patience and a firm technique, but the end result is completely worth the effort. It may not look like the sexiest dish, but this risotto is ultra-rich and hearty without being too heavy.

1. Bring the broth to a boil in a large pot over high heat. Remove the pot from the heat.

2. Heat the olive oil in a medium skillet over medium heat. Add the shallot, and sauté until translucent, about 1 minute.

3. Add the cremini mushrooms, and sauté until they soften and release water, 3 to 5 minutes.

4. Add the garlic, thyme, red pepper flakes, salt, and pepper, and sauté for 1 minute.

5. Add the rice, and toast, gently stirring, for 2 minutes.

6. Add the lemon juice, and sauté for another 30 seconds.

7. Add the warm broth to the risotto, 1 ladle at a time, and cook, stirring gently, until the broth starts to absorb into the rice. Continue adding the broth, stirring continuously, until all the broth is absorbed and the rice is thoroughly cooked, 25 to 30 minutes.

8. Add the Parmesan and butter, turn off the heat, and stir until emulsified.

9. **Make the crispy mushroom topping:** Heat the olive oil in a medium skillet over medium heat. Add the mushrooms, and sear until browned and crispy but still a bit juicy, 5 to 7 minutes. Season with salt and pepper.

10. Garnish the risotto with the crispy mushrooms, a generous portion of fresh Parmesan, and a heavy drizzle of black truffle oil, and serve.

---

5 cups vegetable broth
3 tablespoons olive oil
1 small shallot, finely chopped
4 ounces cremini mushrooms, sliced
2 tablespoons roughly chopped garlic
Leaves from 3 fresh thyme sprigs
½ teaspoon red pepper flakes, or to taste
Salt and black pepper, to taste
1 cup arborio rice
2 teaspoons lemon juice
½ cup freshly grated Parmesan, very loosely packed, plus more for serving
3 tablespoons unsalted butter
Black truffle oil

crispy mushroom topping
2 tablespoons olive oil
4 ounces shiitake, oyster, and cremini mushrooms
Salt and black pepper, to taste

no-fuss black bean burgers

makes 2 burgers

I would never yuck your yum, but I do think adding breadcrumbs to black bean burgers deserves jail time. I, harboring great wisdom beyond my years, have discovered that the perfectly moist (sorry) and juicy black bean burger simply needs eggs and flour in the base. Less is more, or whatever.

1. Heat 1 tablespoon oil in a medium skillet over medium heat. Add the onion and bell pepper, and sauté until the onion is translucent and the bell pepper is slightly softened, about 2 minutes.

2. Add the beans, salt, and pepper, and sauté until the beans start to soften, 3 minutes.

3. Using the back of a spatula, gently smash about one third of the beans. Keep the rest of beans whole to add texture.

4. Transfer the mixture to a large bowl and let cool until just slightly warm, about 5 minutes.

5. Add the flour, garlic powder, chile powder, onion powder, paprika, and egg to the bowl, and mix well. Let the mixture cool until it is comfortable to the touch.

6. Add 1 to 2 tablespoons of oil to your hands and rub them together. (This will prevent the mixture from sticking to your palms.) Divide the black bean mixture in half, and use your hands to form each portion into a patty.

7. Heat the remaining 1 to 2 tablespoons of oil in the medium skillet over medium heat. Reduce the heat to medium-low. Add the burgers, and cook until the first side is crispy and browned, about 2 minutes. Flip over the burgers and cook the other side until crispy and browned, another 2 minutes. Continue cooking and flipping as needed to achieve your desired crispness.

8. Serve the burgers on brioche buns with pepper jack, lettuce, tomato, harissa, and mayonnaise, or your favorite burger toppings.

3 to 5 tablespoons olive oil, divided
¼ large yellow onion, finely chopped
½ red bell pepper, ribs and seeds removed, and finely chopped
One 15-ounce can black beans, rinsed and drained
Salt and black pepper, to taste
½ cup all-purpose flour
½ teaspoon garlic powder
½ teaspoon Kashmiri red chile powder
½ teaspoon onion powder
¼ teaspoon smoked paprika
1 egg

for serving
2 brioche buns
Pepper jack slices
Romaine lettuce leaves
Roma tomato slices
Harissa paste
Mayonnaise

not so meaty

roasted veggie quesadilla

serves 2

Fun fact: If you add veggies to your quesadilla, it's actually healthy now. You're welcome.

1 Heat a large, heavy skillet with a lid over medium-high heat. Add the oil and then add the onion, and sauté for about 30 seconds. Add the garlic, and sauté for 20 seconds.

2 Add the cabbage, bell pepper, and mushrooms. Sprinkle in the salt, pepper, and Cajun seasoning, and stir-fry until the veggies are slightly softened but remain crisp and vibrant in color, about 1 minute. Remove the vegetables from the skillet.

3 If desired, toast the tortillas (otherwise, skip to step 6): Reduce the heat to low and let the skillet cool down. Gently (and carefully) wipe the skillet with a clean paper towel.

4 Add 1 tablespoon butter. It should slightly sizzle and slowly start melting. If the pan is too hot and the butter starts spluttering, remove it from the heat entirely to let it cool.

5 Add half of the hot sauce. It should barely sizzle. Dip both sides of one tortilla in the hot sauce, and move it gently in circular motions to evenly coat. Lightly fry the tortilla in the hot sauce for about 30 seconds per side. Then fry the first side again until it crisps up, another 30 seconds. (This will be the side you place the veggies and cheese on.)

6 Assemble the quesadilla: Lay one tortilla crispy side up in the pan and evenly sprinkle half of the veggies, half of the Mexican cheese blend, and half of the mozzarella on one half of the tortilla. Fold over the quesadilla. Cover the pan, increase the heat to medium-low, and heat the quesadilla for 1 to 2 minutes to melt the cheese evenly.

7 Gently flip over the quesadilla, cover the pan again, and heat for another 1 to 2 minutes. Both sides should be a crispy golden brown.

8 Repeat steps 3 through 7 with the remaining butter, hot sauce, tortilla, veggies, and cheese.

9 Serve with sour cream and pico de gallo.

---

1 tablespoon neutral oil (such as canola or vegetable)
¼ small red onion, thinly sliced
2 large garlic cloves, minced
¼ small head green cabbage, shredded
¼ red bell pepper, ribs and seeds removed, and thinly sliced
¼ green bell pepper, ribs and seeds removed, and thinly sliced
2 baby bella mushrooms, sliced
Salt and black pepper, to taste
1 teaspoon Cajun seasoning
2 large flour tortillas
2 tablespoons salted butter, optional
2 to 3 tablespoons hot sauce (I prefer Valentina or Cholula), divided, optional
⅔ cup shredded Mexican cheese blend
¼ cup shredded mozzarella

for serving
Sour cream
Pico de gallo

make it meatless

cajun corn

serves 2

Sometimes, the best recipes are the simplest! This no-frills Cajun corn is quick and easy and can be whipped up with just a few ingredients. It's ultra buttery and tangy, and it has the perfect amount of kick.

2 tablespoons salted butter
2 ears of corn, husked
1 large lemon

cajun butter

2 to 3 tablespoons salted butter
1 tablespoon Cajun seasoning
1 teaspoon lemon pepper
Salt, to taste

1. Preheat the oven to 450°F.

2. Cut the butter into two pats. Place them side by side on a large sheet of foil. Set the corn on top of the butter, and wrap both tightly in the foil.

3. Place the wrapped corn on the middle rack of the oven, and cook for 20 to 25 minutes, until the corn is juicy and plump. Remove the corn from the foil.

4. **Make the Cajun butter:** Place the butter in a small bowl, and microwave it in 10-second intervals until softened.

5. Add the Cajun seasoning, lemon pepper, and salt, and mix well.

6. Cut the lemon in half, and rub it against the corn, squeezing out the juice as you rub.

7. Brush the Cajun butter over the corn, add more lemon juice if desired, and serve.

not so meaty

tofu bahn mi

serves 2 to 3

A crispy French baguette filled with marinated tofu, homemade pickled daikon and carrots, creamy sriracha mayo, and some fresh herbs. What could be better?

1 **Make the marinated tofu:** Drain and press the tofu for 15 minutes to remove as much water as possible.

2 Combine the light soy sauce, honey, water, Fresno chile, if using, garlic, sesame oil, dark soy sauce, and rice vinegar in a small bowl.

3 Slice the tofu block lengthwise once and widthwise twice to end up with six long rectangular pieces. Cut each piece in half to make 12 skinny rectangular pieces. Place the tofu pieces in an 11 × 7½-inch baking dish or a large, shallow bowl.

4 Pour the marinade over the tofu, and set in the refrigerator to marinate overnight.

5 **Make the pickled carrots and daikon:** Place the water, white vinegar, sugar, red chile, garlic, peppercorns, and salt in a small pot over medium heat. Bring to a soft boil for about 1 minute.

6 Place the carrot and daikon in a small mason jar or heatproof airtight container. Pour the hot liquid mixture over the veggies. Let cool to room temperature, close the lid, and place in the refrigerator overnight.

7 Preheat the oven to 400°F. Line a baking sheet with foil.

8 Remove the tofu from the marinade, gently shake off the excess liquid, and transfer the tofu to the prepared baking sheet. Cook for 25 to 30 minutes, flipping once halfway through, until golden brown.

9 To serve, slice the baguette horizontally and toast it. Add the tofu, and squeeze a little lime juice on top. Add the sriracha mayonnaise, pickled carrots and daikon, cilantro, mint, if using, and jalapeño, and serve.

marinated tofu
- One 15.5-ounce block extra-firm tofu
- ½ cup light soy sauce
- ⅓ cup honey
- ⅓ cup water
- 1½ tablespoons finely chopped Fresno chile (deseeded to reduce heat), optional
- 1½ tablespoons finely chopped garlic
- 1½ tablespoons sesame oil
- 1 tablespoon dark soy sauce
- 1 tablespoon rice vinegar or mirin

spicy pickled daikon and carrots
- 2 cups water
- 2 cups white vinegar
- ¼ cup sugar
- 1 large red chile, sliced
- 5 garlic cloves, sliced
- 1 tablespoon black peppercorns
- 2 teaspoons salt
- 1 large carrot, julienned
- ½ daikon radish, julienned

for serving
- 1 French baguette
- Lime wedges
- Sriracha mayonnaise
- Chopped fresh cilantro
- Chopped fresh mint, optional
- Thinly sliced jalapeño

make it meatless

note
If you don't have an air fryer, you can pan-fry the paneer in about 2 tablespoons canola oil over medium heat for 4 to 5 minutes per side.

paneer kathi rolls

serves 2

Indian food is truly the best reminder that vegetarian food isn't all bland and boring. These mouthwatering paneer kathi rolls are ultra-spicy and bursting with flavor. The seasoned paneer is garnished with chiles soaked in vinegar, spicy sautéed pickled onions, a cool yogurt chutney, and crispy red cabbage. Are you drooling yet?

1 Preheat an air fryer to 350°F. Place the chiles and vinegar in a small bowl, and set aside to marinate.

2 **Make the paneer:** Combine the yogurt, besan, chile powder, cumin, coriander, fenugreek, amchur, chaat masala, garam masala, salt, and turmeric in a large bowl.

3 Cut the paneer into rectangular pieces about 1 inch wide and 2 inches long. Add the paneer to the yogurt mixture, and toss to coat.

4 Fry the paneer in the air fryer for about 15 minutes, flipping halfway through the cook time, until the yogurt is completely dried and the paneer is slightly crisped (see Note).

5 **Make the chutney:** Place the yogurt, cilantro, chiles, lemon juice, mint, amchur, chaat masala, cumin, garlic powder, and salt in a high-speed blender, and blend until smooth.

6 **Make the pickled onions:** Heat the oil in a small skillet over medium heat. Add the onion, and sauté until softened, 2 to 3 minutes.

7 Add the lime juice, and sauté until some of the lime juice absorbs into the onion and the onion turns bright pink, another 30 seconds.

8 Add the chaat masala and chile powder, and continue sautéing until the lime juice is completely absorbed into the onions and they have wilted entirely, about 2 minutes.

9 Heat a medium skillet over medium heat.

10 Mix the butter and hot sauce in a small bowl. Coat each tortilla with the butter and hot sauce mixture. Add the tortillas to the skillet, one at a time, and cook until the sauce has dried and the tortilla is slightly crisped on both sides, about 1 minute per side.

11 Add the paneer, chutney, pickled onions, vinegar-soaked chiles, and shredded cabbage to the center of each tortilla, roll into a wrap, and serve.

- 6 Thai green chiles, sliced
- 2 tablespoons distilled white vinegar
- 3 tablespoons salted butter, melted
- 3 tablespoons hot sauce
- 2 large flour tortillas or lachha parathas
- ¼ cup shredded red cabbage

paneer
- 5 tablespoons whole-milk yogurt
- 2 tablespoons besan (chickpea flour)
- 1 teaspoon Kashmiri red chile powder
- ¾ teaspoon ground cumin
- ½ teaspoon ground coriander
- ½ teaspoon dried fenugreek leaves
- ¼ teaspoon amchur (mango powder)
- ¼ teaspoon chaat masala
- ¼ teaspoon garam masala
- ¼ teaspoon salt
- ¼ teaspoon ground turmeric
- 8 ounces paneer

chutney
- ¼ cup whole-milk yogurt
- 3 tablespoons finely chopped fresh cilantro, tightly packed
- 2 Thai green chiles
- 1 tablespoon lemon juice
- 1 tablespoon finely chopped fresh mint, tightly packed
- ⅛ teaspoon amchur (mango powder)
- ⅛ teaspoon chaat masala
- ⅛ teaspoon ground cumin
- ⅛ teaspoon garlic powder
- ⅛ teaspoon salt

instant pickled onions
- 1 tablespoon canola oil
- ¼ large red onion, sliced
- Juice of 1 lime
- ¾ teaspoon chaat masala
- ¾ teaspoon Kashmiri red chile powder

not so meaty

quick

Mix and match the elements of various recipes in this book to create something brand new! The meats, sauces, marinades, and sides in this book are all so versatile, so this chapter will give you some ideas on how to use them to make your own custom recipes.

buffalo chicken grilled cheese

serves 2

Here's a delicious take on the classic grilled cheese we all know and love! Tangy Buffalo sauce, gooey mozzarella, and Chicken 2.0 (page 21) as the base–what more could a girl ask for?

- ¼ batch Chicken 2.0 (page 21), torn into bite-size pieces
- 2 to 4 tablespoons Buffalo sauce, to taste
- 4 large slices sourdough bread
- 1 cup shredded mozzarella
- ¼ cup mayonnaise
- 4 tablespoons salted butter, melted
- Ranch dressing

1. Place the chicken in a medium bowl, pour the Buffalo sauce over the top, and mix to coat.

2. Evenly divide and spread the chicken on one side of two slices of bread. Cover with the mozzarella. Place the other slices of bread on top, and press firmly.

3. Mix the mayonnaise and butter in a small bowl. Spread the mixture evenly on both sides of the outside of the sandwiches.

4. Place the sandwiches in a medium skillet over medium heat, and cook until the outsides are crispy and golden brown and the cheese is melted on the inside, about 3 minutes per side. (I recommend covering the skillet to create steam and help the cheese melt through the center.)

5. Serve with ranch dressing.

birria ramen

serves 2

I know fusion food has some haters, but if combining your favorite foods into one super dish is wrong, then I don't wanna be right. Birria ramen is simply everything I love about food. Rich, spicy, cheesy noodles with meaty shrooms—what more could you ask for?

1. Cook the ramen noodles according to the package instructions. Rinse with cold water and drain.

2. Divide the broth, meat, and noodles between two small bowls.

3. Top with scallions, cilantro, onion, and cheese. Season with salt and pepper, and serve with lime wedges on the side.

Two 3-ounce packets instant ramen
½ batch birria broth (see Birria Tacos, page 90)
½ batch birria meat (see Birria Tacos, page 90)

for serving
Chopped scallions
Chopped fresh cilantro
Chopped yellow onion
Shredded Oaxaca cheese
Salt and black pepper, to taste
Lime wedges

chili cheese dogs
serves 4

The only part of baseball games that has ever been appealing to me is the food: popcorn, warm pretzels, and of course, the mighty chili cheese dog. Now you can skip the sports stadium and go straight to the good stuff with these rich and cheesy dogs made from scratch, right at home. (Have the game on in the background, or whatever, if that's your thing.)

1 Toast the hot dog buns until golden brown.

2 Place the hot dogs in the buns. Cover with the chili and then add the cheese sauce on top.

3 Garnish with pickled jalapeños, red onion, and cilantro, and serve.

4 large hot dog buns
1 batch Hot Dogs (page 30)
½ cup Chili (page 106), divided
½ cup cheese sauce (see Chicken Nachos, page 115), divided

for serving
Pickled jalapeños
Finely chopped red onion
Finely chopped fresh cilantro

meatball sliders

makes 8 sliders

These cheesy, saucy, and lush meatball sliders are sure to be a crowd pleaser! You can use any flavor of leftover meatballs to create this quick and easy recipe.

1. Preheat the oven to 350°F.
2. Slice the Hawaiian rolls in half horizontally, and place the bottom halves on a baking sheet. Spread the pesto, if using, evenly on the insides of both halves of the rolls.
3. Add one meatball to the bottom half of each roll.
4. Pour a few tablespoons of the marinara sauce over each meatball, enough to coat each meatball evenly.
5. Sprinkle the mozzarella and Parmesan evenly over the meatballs.
6. Place the top halves of the Hawaiian rolls back on, and gently press down.
7. Mix the butter and garlic in a small bowl. Use a basting brush to spread the garlic butter evenly over the tops of the rolls.
8. Cover the baking sheet with foil, and bake the sliders for 10 to 15 minutes, until the cheese is melted and the meatballs are warmed through.
9. Sprinkle with parsley, and serve.

- 8 Hawaiian rolls
- ½ cup Cashew Truffle Oil Pesto (page 249), optional
- 1 batch Meatballs (page 34)
- ½ cup marinara sauce (store-bought or from Chicken Parmesan, page 155)
- ½ cup shredded mozzarella
- ¼ cup freshly grated Parmesan
- 3 tablespoons salted butter, melted
- 2 garlic cloves, minced
- Chopped fresh parsley leaves, to taste

wing platter

serves 6 to 9

You'll no longer have to suffer the gross injustice of eating only celery and carrot sticks at your family barbecue or a game-day gathering. Bring this delicious wing platter to satiate you instead! (And don't share it with them if the only vegetarian option they ever had for you was celery and carrots. Stay petty.)

1 Use a basting brush to evenly coat each wing in about ¼ cup of the sauce of your choice.

2 Serve.

3 batches Classic Fried Chicken (page 27), formed into wing shapes in step 2

recommended sauces
Buffalo sauce
Barbecue sauce
Gochujang Sauce (page 248)
Teriyaki Sauce (page 249), with sesame seeds for garnish
Hot Honey (page 248)
Bang Bang Sauce (page 246), with chopped fresh parsley for garnish

barbecue chicken wraps

serves 2

When I was in college, Trader Joe's sold a vegan barbecue chicken wrap that has since been discontinued (as a personal slight toward me, I think). I used to walk more than 30 minutes away from campus to get this wrap. My point is that I will go to great lengths (literally) for good food. That's why I went out of my way to develop this recipe to fill the barbecue chicken wrap–shaped hole in my heart.

- 1 batch Classic Fried Chicken (page 27), prepared through step 1
- 2 large flour tortillas
- ¼ cup barbecue sauce
- 1 to 2 cups shredded iceberg lettuce, loosely packed, to taste
- 1 Roma tomato, chopped
- ¼ small red onion, chopped
- ¼ cup shredded cheddar
- Blue cheese dressing

1. Break the mushrooms for the Classic Fried Chicken into about 12 bite-size pieces. Proceed with step 3 of that recipe and then reduce the frying time to 3 to 4 minutes in step 5. (The smaller pieces fry more quickly.)

2. Heat a medium skillet over medium heat. Add the tortillas, one at a time, and cook until they are warmed all the way through, about 30 seconds per side.

3. Coat the chicken evenly in the barbecue sauce, and add half to the center of each tortilla. Top each with half of the lettuce, tomato, red onion, and cheddar, and roll each into a wrap.

4. Serve with blue cheese dressing.

bang bang chicken

serves 2 to 5

Crispy fried chicken slathered in a mouthwatering sweet chili mayo sauce and topped with chopped parsley. *Chef's kiss.*

1 batch Classic Fried Chicken (page 27; see Note)
Bang Bang Sauce (page 246)
Chopped fresh parsley

1. Evenly coat the chicken with a generous layer of the bang bang sauce.

2. Garnish with parsley, and serve.

note

When making the Classic Fried Chicken, add 1 tablespoon of sriracha sauce to the wet batter and remove the cumin from both the wet and dry batters. Then form the mushrooms into wing shapes in step 2.

make it meatless

When it comes to sauce, I've always said more is more. Sneak a peek at my favorite sauces, glazes, and dips that add the perfect finishing touch to any recipe.

saucy

thai sweet chili sauce

makes about 2 cups

This delectable Thai sweet chili sauce is the perfect accompaniment for crab rangoons, spring rolls, wings, and even fries! It also works wonderfully as a glaze on a crispy fried chicken burger.

2¼ cups water, divided
10 small garlic cloves
6 Thai red chiles
1 cup sugar
2 tablespoons white vinegar
1 tablespoon ketchup
1 tablespoon soy sauce
1 teaspoon salt
2 tablespoons cornstarch

1. Place the 2 cups water, garlic, and chiles in a high-speed blender, and blend until smooth.

2. Add the sugar, vinegar, ketchup, soy sauce, and salt.

3. Transfer the sauce to a small saucepan over medium heat, bring to a simmer, and cook for about 5 minutes.

4. Create a cornstarch slurry by whisking the cornstarch and the remaining ¼ cup water until no lumps remain.

5. Add the slurry to the sauce, and simmer until the sauce starts to thicken and has the consistency of maple syrup, 5 minutes. Remove from the heat and let cool. The sauce should thicken further to a honey-like consistency.

6. Let cool and then store in an airtight container in the refrigerator for up to 1 week.

bang bang sauce

makes about ½ cup

This bang bang sauce pairs perfectly with wings, chicken nuggets, and karaage. It also makes a great spread for sandwiches and burgers.

¼ cup Kewpie mayonnaise
2 to 3 tablespoons Thai Sweet Chili Sauce (see above), to taste
1 tablespoon sriracha
1 teaspoon mirin

1. Combine the mayonnaise, sweet chili sauce, sriracha, and mirin in a small bowl.

2. Store in an airtight container in the refrigerator for up to 4 days.

tartar sauce
makes about ½ cup

Serve this creamy and vibrant tartar sauce with fried fish, fish tacos, calamari, and even fries.

1. Combine the mayonnaise, dill pickle, garlic, capers, chives, lemon juice, mustard, salt, pepper, onion powder, and hot sauce in a small bowl.

2. Store in an airtight container in the refrigerator for up to 4 days.

- ¼ cup Kewpie mayonnaise
- 1 tablespoon finely chopped dill pickle
- 1 garlic clove, minced
- ½ teaspoon capers
- ½ teaspoon finely chopped fresh chives
- ½ teaspoon lemon juice
- ½ teaspoon Dijon mustard
- Salt and black pepper, to taste
- ⅛ teaspoon onion powder
- Dash of Louisiana hot sauce

green chutney
makes about ¾ cup

Drizzle this green chutney over tandoori chicken rolls, kathi rolls, aloo frankies, or chaat papri, or use it as a dip for samosas and pakoras. You can also add this to a cucumber, tomato, mayo, and butter sandwich for some extra spice and flavor. (Don't forget to add some chaat masala if you do.)

1. Place the cilantro, mint, green chiles, yogurt, garlic, ginger, salt, and cumin in a high-speed blender, and blend until smooth, about 30 to 60 seconds. You may need to add 1 to 2 tablespoons water to help the blending process.

2. Store in an airtight container in the refrigerator for up to 5 days.

- 1 bunch fresh cilantro, leaves and stems
- 0.5 ounce fresh mint leaves
- 4 Thai green chiles (deseeded for less of a kick)
- 2 tablespoons Greek yogurt
- 2 garlic cloves
- ½ inch ginger
- 1 teaspoon salt
- ¾ teaspoon ground cumin

gochujang sauce

makes about ⅓ cup

This sweet and spicy gochujang sauce is perfect for burgers and wings. It's also great as a dipping sauce for tortilla chips! (Trust me on this.)

- ¼ cup gochujang paste
- 1 tablespoon plus 1 teaspoon honey
- 2 teaspoons soy sauce
- 1 teaspoon rice vinegar
- 1 teaspoon toasted sesame oil

1. Mix the gochujang, honey, soy sauce, vinegar, and sesame oil in a small bowl until evenly combined.
2. Store in an airtight container in the refrigerator for up to 1 week.

chipotle sauce

makes about 1 cup

Use this chipotle sauce to add a spicy and creamy touch to tacos, burritos, or quesadillas. It also works well as a drizzle over nachos or as a dipping sauce for fries.

- ½ cup mayonnaise
- ¼ cup sour cream
- 2 tablespoons canned chipotle peppers in adobo sauce
- 1 teaspoon rice vinegar
- 2 garlic cloves
- ½ teaspoon onion powder
- ½ teaspoon salt
- ¼ teaspoon smoked paprika

1. Place the mayonnaise, sour cream, chipotles, vinegar, garlic, onion powder, salt, and paprika in a high-speed blender, and blend until combined, 15 to 30 seconds.
2. Store in an airtight container in the refrigerator for up to 4 days.

hot honey

makes about ⅔ cup

Slather this hot honey on some fried chicken wings, use it as a dipping sauce for fries or chicken nuggets, or drizzle some on top of your favorite flatbreads.

- ⅔ cup honey
- 2 tablespoons hot sauce (I like Cholula)
- 1 teaspoon cayenne

1. Combine the honey, hot sauce, and cayenne in a small bowl.
2. Store in an airtight container at room temperature for up to 1 week.

teriyaki sauce

makes about ⅔ cup

The perfect teriyaki stir-fry sauce is here! Use this to coat your meatless meats, noods, or veg.

- ¼ cup soy sauce
- 3 tablespoons brown sugar
- 2 tablespoons sriracha
- 2 tablespoons honey
- 1 tablespoon rice vinegar
- 1 tablespoon sesame oil
- 1 teaspoon sesame seeds
- 2 tablespoons water
- 1 teaspoon cornstarch

1. Combine the soy sauce, brown sugar, sriracha, honey, vinegar, sesame oil, and sesame seeds in a small bowl.

2. Create a cornstarch slurry by combining the water and cornstarch in a separate small bowl. Add the slurry to the sauce, and mix well.

3. Transfer to a small saucepan, and heat over medium-low heat. Simmer until the sauce starts to thicken and has the consistency of maple syrup, 1 to 2 minutes. Mix continuously with a silicone spatula to prevent clumping.

4. Let cool and then store in an airtight container in the refrigerator for up to 1 week.

cashew truffle oil pesto

makes about 1 cup

Add this pesto to pastas, pizzas, and sandwiches. You can also spruce up your sunny-side-up eggs by drizzling some of this pesto on top. She's versatile.

- 3 ounces fresh basil leaves
- 6 tablespoons olive oil
- ¼ cup unsalted cashews
- ¼ cup freshly grated Parmesan
- 1 tablespoon lemon juice, optional
- 4 garlic cloves
- 1 tablespoon white truffle oil
- ½ to 1 teaspoon salt, to taste
- Black pepper, to taste

1. Place the basil, olive oil, cashews, Parmesan, lemon juice, garlic, truffle oil, salt, and pepper in a food processor or blender, and blend for about 30 seconds to form a smooth paste.

2. Store in an airtight container in the refrigerator for up to 5 days.

index

A

aborio rice, in Mushroom Risotto, 212
Asparagus, Steak with Garlic-Chive Butter and, 168–169
avocado
    Ceviche, 120
    Fish Tacos, 184

B

Bacon
    BLT, 201
    recipe, 38
Bacon Bits
    Bucatini Carbonara, 75
    recipe, 38
bamboo shoots
    Pad Kee Mao, 67
    Thai Chicken Red Curry, 98
banana blossoms, 13
    Blackened Fish, 180
    Fish and Chips, 187
    Fish Tacos, 184
    Marinated and Battered Fish, 36
Bang Bang Sauce
    Bang Bang Chicken, 240
    recipe, 246
    Wing Platter, 236
barbecue sauce
    Barbecue Chicken Wraps, 239
    Pulled Pork Sandwiches, 52
    Wing Platter, 236
basil leaves. *See also* Thai basil leaves
    Cashew Truffle Oil Pesto, 249
    Chicken Parmesan, 155
    Italian Meatball Soup, 105
    Pesto Caprese Sandwiches, 56
    Sausage Rigatoni, 72
    Thai Chicken Red Curry, 98
beans
    Beef, 28–29
    Chicken 2.0, 21
    Chili, 106
    No-Fuss Black Bean Burgers, 215
bean sprouts
    Chicken Chow Mein, 76
    Chicken Pad Thai, 64
    Chicken Pho, 101
Beef
    Beef and Broccoli, 147
    Mongolian Beef, 135
    Philly Cheesesteaks, 59
    recipe, 28–29
beef, good substitutes for, 13
beaetroot powder, 14
    Beef, 28–29
    Steak with Chimichurri, 171
    Steak with Garlic-Chive Butter and Asparagus, 168–169
bell peppers
    Chicken Fajitas, 86
    Chicken Taquitos, 119
    Chili, 106
    Gumbo, 102
    No-Fuss Black Bean Burgers, 215
    Pad Kee Mao, 67
    Roasted Veggie Quesadilla, 216
    Sausage and Peppers, 205
    Thai Chicken Red Curry, 98
The Best Frozen Tofu Technique, 39
birria meat
    Birria Ramen, 231
    Birria Tacos, 90
Blackened Fish, 180
BLT, 201
bread(s). *See also* naan bread
    Buffalo Chicken Grilled Cheese, 228
    Sausage Flatbread with Truffle Pesto, 198
    Tofu Bahn Mi, 220
broccoli
    Beef and Broccoli, 147
    Pad Kee Mao, 67
bucatini
    Bucatini Carbonara, 75
    Creamy Sun-Dried Tomato Pasta, 68
Buffalo sauce
    Buffalo Burgers, 48
    Buffalo Chicken Grilled Cheese, 228
    Buffalo Chicken Snack Wraps, 51
    Wing Platter, 236
buns and rolls
    Buffalo Burgers, 48
    Chili Cheese Dogs, 232
    Crispy Fish Sandwiches with Tartar Sauce, 55
    Gochujang Chicken Sandwiches, 44
    Hot Honey Chicken Rolls, 160
    Korean Fried Chicken Bao, 92–93
    Meatball Sliders, 235
    No-Fuss Black Bean Burgers, 215
    Pesto Caprese Sandwiches, 56
    Philly Cheesesteaks, 59
    Pulled Pork Sandwiches, 52
    Shroom Burger, 47
    Tandoori Chicken Rolls, 172
burgers
    Buffalo Burgers, 48
    No-Fuss Black Bean Burgers, 215
    Shroom Burger, 47
Butter Chicken, 144

C

cabbage
    Chicken Chow Mein, 76
    Chicken Pad Thai, 64
    Chipotle Chicken Tacos, 116
    Fish Tacos, 184
    Hot Honey Chicken Rolls, 160
    Korean Fried Chicken Bao, 92–93
    Paneer Kathi Rolls, 223
    Roasted Veggie Quesadilla, 216
    Spicy Wontons, 143
Cajun seasoning
    Blackened Fish, 180
    Cajun Corn, 219
    Gumbo, 102
    Roasted Veggie Quesadilla, 216
Carnitas Tacos, 85
carrots. *See also* pickled daikon and carrots
    Chicken Chow Mein, 76
    Chicken Pad Thai, 63
    Chicken Pho, 101
    Hot Honey Chicken Rolls, 160
    Tofu Bahn Mi, 220
Cashew Truffle Oil Pesto
    Meatball Sliders, 235
    recipe, 249
    Sausage Flatbread with Truffle Pesto, 198

make it meatless

celery
- Chicken Pho, 101
- Crab Cakes, 183
- Gumbo, 102

Ceviche, 120
char siu sauce, in Pork Buns, 206–207
cheddar cheese
- Barbecue Chicken Wraps, 239
- Buffalo Chicken Snack Wraps, 51
- Chicken Taquitos, 119
- Chili, 106

cheese. *See also* cheddar cheese; Mexican cheese blend; Monterey Jack cheese; mozzarella cheese; Parmesan cheese
- American, in Crispy Fish Sandwiches with Tartar Sauce, 55
- pepper jack, in Chicken Taquitos, 119
- provolone, Philly Cheesesteaks, 59

cheese sauce
- Chicken Nachos, 115
- Chili Cheese Dogs, 232

Chicken 1.0
- Chicken Fajitas, 86
- recipe, 20

Chicken 2.0
- adding to Pad Kee Mao, 67
- Buffalo Chicken Grilled Cheese, 228
- Butter Chicken, 144
- Chicken Fried Rice, 139
- Chicken Nachos, 115
- Chicken Pho, 101
- Chicken Quesadillas, 132
- Chili Chicken, 89
- Chipotle Chicken Tacos, 116
- Pesto Caprese Sandwiches, 56
- recipe, 21
- Thai Chicken Red Curry, 98

Chicken 3.0
- Chicken Pad Thai, 64
- Orange Chicken, 131
- recipe, 24
- Teriyaki Chicken, 128

Chicken and Waffles, 163
Chicken Chow Mein, 76
Chicken Fajitas, 86
Chicken Fried Rice, 139
chicken, good substitutes for, 13
Chicken Nachos, 115
Chicken Nuggets, 152
Chicken Pad Thai, 64
Chicken Parmesan, 155
Chicken Pho, 101
Chicken Quesadillas, 132
Chicken Taquitos, 119

chickpeas, in Steak with Garlic-Chive Butter and Asparagus, 168–169
Chili, 106
Chili Cheese Dogs, 232
Chili Chicken, 89
Chimichangas, 136
Chimichurri, Steak with, 171
Chinese broccoli, in Pad Kee Mao, 67
Chipotle Chicken Tacos, 116
chipotle peppers
- Chicken Nachos, 115
- Chipotle Chicken Tacos, 116
- Chipotle Sauce, 248

Chipotle Sauce
- Chicken Quesadillas, 132
- Chicken Taquitos, 119
- Chipotle Chicken Tacos, 116
- recipe, 248

chow mein noodles, in Chicken Chow Mein, 76
chutney, in Paneer Kathi Rolls, 223. *See also* Green Chutney
Classic Fried Chicken
- Bang Bang Chicken, 240
- Barbecue Chicken Wraps, 239
- Buffalo Chicken Snack Wraps, 51
- Chicken and Waffles, 163
- recipe, 26–27
- Wing Platter, 236

coconut milk, in Thai Chicken Red Curry, 98
coleslaw
- Hot Honey Chicken Rolls, 160
- Pulled Pork Sandwiches, 52

color, ingredients for, 14
Corn, Cajun, 219
corn, canned, in Chicken Taquitos, 119
Corn Dogs, Korean, 82
Crab Cakes, 183
Crab Rangoon, 188
cream cheese
- Chicken Taquitos, 119
- Crab Rangoon, 188

Creamy Sun-Dried Tomato Pasta, 68
cremini mushrooms, in Mushroom Risotto, 212
Crispy Fish Sandwiches with Tartar Sauce, 55
curry paste, in Thai Chicken Red Curry, 98

D

Deli Ham, 22
dill, fresh
- Creamy Sun-Dried Tomato Pasta, 68
- Gyros, 175

E

egg(s)
- Bucatini Carbonara, 75
- Chicken and Waffles, 163
- Fried Calamari, 191
- Pad Kra Pao, 202

Enchiladas, 123
enoki mushrooms
- about, 13
- Crispy Fish Sandwiches with Tartar Sauce, 55
- Enoki Mushroom Fried Chicken, 156

equipment, kitchen, 16

F

Fajitas, Chicken, 86
fenugreek leaves
- Butter Chicken, 144
- Paneer Kathi Rolls, 223
- Tandoori Chicken Rolls, 172

Fish and Chips, 187
fish, good substitute for, 13
Fish Tacos, 184
Fishy Batter
- Crispy Fish Sandwiches with Tartar Sauce, 55
- Marinated and Battered Fish, 36

Fishy Marinade
- Blackened Fish, 180
- Marinated and Battered Fish, 36

flatbread, Sausage Flatbread with Truffle Pesto, 198
flour tortillas. *See* tortillas
Fried Calamari, 191
fried chicken. *See* Classic Fried Chicken
Fried Chicken, Enoki Mushroom, 156
frozen vegetables, Chicken Fried Rice, 139

G

Gochujang Chicken Sandwiches, 44
gochujang paste
- Enoki Mushroom Fried Chicken, 156

index   251

Gochujang Chicken Sandwiches, 44
Gochujang Sauce, 248
Korean Fried Chicken Bao, 92–93
Gochujang Sauce
   recipe, 248
   Wing Platter, 236
Greek yogurt
   Green Chutney, 247
   Gyros, 175
   Tandoori Chicken Rolls, 172
Green Chutney
   recipe, 247
   Tandoori Chicken Rolls, 172
ground beef/pork, substitute for, 13
Gyros, 175

H

honey. *See* Hot Honey
Hot Dogs
   Chili Cheese Dogs, 232
   Korean Corn Dogs, 82
   recipe, 30
Hot Honey
   Hot Honey Chicken Rolls, 160
   recipe, 248
   Wing Platter, 236

I

Italian Meatballs
   Italian Meatball Soup, 105
   Meatball Sliders, 235
   recipe, 34

J

jackfruit, 13
   Carnitas Tacos, 85
   Chimichangas, 136

K

Karaage, 164
Kewpie mayonnaise
   Bang Bang Sauce, 246
   Crab Cakes, 183
   Karaage, 164
   Tartar Sauce, 247
kimchi slaw, in Gochujang Chicken Sandwiches, 44
king oyster mushrooms, 13
   Birria Tacos, 90
   Ceviche, 120

Crab Rangoon, 188
Creamy Sun-Dried Tomato Pasta, 68
Fried Calamari, 191
Parmesan Orzo with Brown Butter Scallops, 192
Pork Buns, 206–207
Pulled Pork Sandwiches, 52
Sesame Scallops, 112
kombu, in Marinated and Battered Fish, 36
Korean Corn Dogs, 82
Korean Fried Chicken Bao, 92–93

L

lemongrass stalks, in Thai Chicken Red Curry, 98
lettuce
   Barbecue Chicken Wraps, 239
   BLT, 201
   Buffalo Chicken Snack Wraps, 51
   Crispy Fish Sandwiches with Tartar Sauce, 55
   Gyros, 175
   No-Fuss Black Bean Burgers, 215
   Shroom Burger, 47
lion's mane mushrooms, 13
   Chicken Chow Mein, 76
   Crab Cakes, 183
   Steak with Chimichurri, 171
liquid smoke
   Bacon, 38
   Carnitas Tacos, 85
   Gyros, 175
   Pad Kra Pao, 202
   Pork Buns, 206–207
   Pulled Pork Sandwiches, 52
   Steak with Chimichurri, 171
   Steak with Garlic-Chive Butter and Asparagus, 168–169
   Tan Tan Ramen, 71

M

maple syrup, in Chicken and Waffles, 163
marinara sauce
   Chicken Parmesan, 155
   Meatball Sliders, 235
Marinated and Battered Fish
   Fish and Chips, 187
   Fish Tacos, 184
   recipe, 36
meatballs. *See* Italian Meatballs
Meatball Sliders, 235

Meat Crumbles
   Chili, 106
   Enchiladas, 123
   recipe, 33
   Spicy Wontons, 143
meat substitutes
   reasons for using, 8–9
   types of, 13
Mexican cheese blend
   Chicken Quesadillas, 132
   Enchiladas, 123
   Roasted Veggie Quesadilla, 216
miso paste
   The Best Frozen Tofu Technique, 39
   Chicken 2.0, 21
   Chicken 3.0, 24
   Steak with Chimichurri, 171
   Tan Tan Ramen, 71
Mongolian Beef, 135
Monterey Jack cheese
   Chicken Nachos, 115
   Chimichangas, 136
   Chipotle Chicken Tacos, 116
mozzarella cheese
   Buffalo Chicken Grilled Cheese, 228
   Chicken Parmesan, 155
   Korean Corn Dogs, 82
   Meatball Sliders, 235
   Pesto Caprese Sandwiches, 56
   Roasted Veggie Quesadilla, 216
   Sausage Flatbread with Truffle Pesto, 198
   Shroom Burger, 47
Mushroom Risotto, 212
mushrooms. *See also* king oyster mushrooms; oyster mushrooms
   Mushroom Risotto, 212
   Roasted Veggie Quesadilla, 216
   Shroom Burger, 47

N

naan bread. *See also* buns and rolls
   Sausage Flatbread with Truffle Pesto, 198
   Tandoori Chicken Rolls, 172
Nachos, Chicken, 115
Nashville Hot Chicken Tenders
   Hot Honey Chicken Rolls, 160
   recipe, 159
No-Fuss Black Bean Burgers, 215
noodles. *See also* pasta dishes; ramen noodles; rice noodles
   Chicken Chow Mein, 76
   Chicken Pho, 101
nutritional yeast
   Beef, 28

252 make it meatless

The Best Frozen Tofu
    Technique, 39
Chicken Pho, 101
Enchiladas, 123
Steak with Garlic-Chive Butter
    and Asparagus, 168–169
nuts
    Butter Chicken, 143
    Cashew Truffle Oil Pesto, 249
    Chicken Pad Thai, 64
    Pesto Caprese Sandwiches, 56

O

Oaxaca cheese
    Birria Ramen, 231
    Birria Tacos, 90
Orange Chicken, 131
orzo, in Parmesan Orzo with Brown
    Butter Scallops, 192
oyster mushrooms, 13. See also king
    oyster mushrooms
    Bacon, 38
    Ceviche, 120
    Classic Fried Chicken, 26–27
    Crab Rangoon, 188
    Gyros, 175
    Karaage, 164
    Korean Fried Chicken Bao,
        92–93
    Mushroom Risotto, 212
    Nashville Hot Chicken Tenders,
        159
    Tandoori Chicken Rolls, 172

P

Pad Kee Mao, 67
Pad Kra Pao, 202
paneer, in Paneer Kathi Rolls, 223
panko bread crumbs
    Buffalo Burgers, 48
    Chicken Nuggets, 152
    Chicken Parmesan, 155
    Classic Fried Chicken, 26–27
    Crab Cakes, 183
    Gochujang Chicken
        Sandwiches, 44
    Korean Corn Dogs, 82
    Nashville Hot Chicken Tenders,
        159
    Shroom Burger, 47
pantry ingredients, 14
Parmesan cheese
    Bucatini Carbonara, 75
    Cashew Truffle Oil Pesto, 249
    Chicken Parmesan, 155

Creamy Sun-Dried Tomato
    Pasta, 68
Italian Meatball Soup, 105
Meatball Sliders, 235
Mushroom Risotto, 212
Parmesan Orzo with Brown
    Butter Scallops, 192
Pesto Caprese Sandwiches, 56
Sausage Flatbread with Truffle
    Pesto, 198
Sausage Rigatoni, 72
pasta dishes
    Bucatini Carbonara, 75
    Creamy Sun-Dried Tomato
        Pasta, 68
    Parmesan Orzo with Brown
        Butter Scallops, 192
    Sausage Rigatoni, 72
peanut butter, in Tan Tan Ramen,
    71
pesto. See Cashew Truffle Oil Pesto
Pesto Caprese Sandwiches, 56
Philly Cheesesteaks, 59
pho noodles, in Chicken Pho, 101
pickled daikon and carrots
    Korean Fried Chicken Bao, 92
    Tofu Bahn Mi, 220
pickled onions
    Gyros, 175
    Paneer Kathi Rolls, 223
    Pesto Caprese Sandwiches, 56
pico de gallo
    Chicken Nachos, 115
    Chicken Taquitos, 119
    Chimichangas, 136
    Chipotle Chicken Tacos, 116
    Roasted Veggie Quesadilla, 216
pine nuts, in Pesto Caprese
    Sandwiches, 56
pita bread, in Gyros, 175
Pork Buns, 206–207
pork, good substitutes for, 13
potatoes, in Fish and Chips, 187
potato starch
    Karaage, 164
    Korean Fried Chicken Bao,
        92–93
prik nam pla sauce, in Pad Kra Pao,
    202
Pulled Pork Sandwiches, 52

Q

QR codes, 10
quesadillas
    Chicken Quesadilla, 132
    Roasted Veggie Quesadilla, 216

R

ramen noodles
    Birria Ramen, 231
    Tan Tan Ramen, 71
red gel food coloring, 14
    Chili Chicken, 89
    Deli Ham, 22
    Hot Dogs, 30
    Sausage, 31
    Tandoori Chicken Rolls, 172
rice
    Beef and Broccoli, 147
    Chicken Fried Rice, 139
    Chili Chicken, 89
    Gumbo, 102
    Mongolian Beef, 135
    Mushroom Risotto, 212
    Orange Chicken, 131
    Pad Kra Pao, 202
    Teriyaki Chicken, 128
    Thai Chicken Red Curry, 98
rice noodles
    Chicken Pad Thai, 64
    Pad Kee Mao, 67
Rigatoni, Sausage, 72
Risotto, Mushroom, 212
Roasted Veggie Quesadilla, 216
rolls. See buns and rolls
romaine lettuce. See lettuce

S

salsa, in Sofritas, 140. See also pico
    de gallo
sandwiches. See also burgers
    BLT, 201
    Buffalo Chicken Grilled Cheese,
        228
    Crispy Fish Sandwiches with
        Tartar Sauce, 55
    Gochujang Chicken
        Sandwiches, 44
    Meatball Sliders, 235
    Pesto Caprese Sandwiches, 56
    Pulled Pork Sandwiches, 52
Sausage
    Gumbo, 102
    recipe, 31
    Sausage and Peppers, 205
    Sausage Flatbread with Truffle
        Pesto, 198
Sausage Crumbles
    recipe, 31
    Sausage Rigatoni, 72
seaweed
    Marinated and Battered Fish,
        36
    Pad Kra Pao, 202

index 253

seitan, 13
seitan beef. *See* Beef
seitan chicken. *See* Chicken 1.0; Chicken 2.0; Chicken 3.0
Shroom Burger, 47
Sofritas, 140
scups
    Chicken Pho, 101
    Gumbo, 102
    Italian Meatball Soup, 105
sour cream
    Chicken Quesadillas, 132
    Chicken Taquitos, 119
    Chili, 106
    Chimichangas, 136
    Chipotle Sauce, 248
    Roasted Veggie Quesadilla, 216
spice blends, 14
spices, 14
spicy sauces, 14
Spicy Wontons, 143
spinach, in Sausage Rigatoni, 72
sriracha
    Chicken Fried Rice, 139
    Chicken Pho, 101
    Chili Chicken, 89
    Fish Tacos, 184
    Karaage, 164
    Mongolian Beef, 135
    Tan Tan Ramen, 71
    Teriyaki Chicken, 128
    Teriyaki Sauce, 249
Steak with Chimichurri, 171
Steak with Garlic-Chive Butter and Asparagus, 168–169
sun-dried tomatoes
    Creamy Sun-Dried Tomato Pasta, 68
    Pesto Caprese Sandwiches, 56
    Sausage Flatbread with Truffle Pesto, 198

T

tacos
    Birria Tacos, 90
    Carnitas Tacos, 85
    Chipotle Chicken Tacos, 116
    Fish Tacos, 184
Tandoori Chicken Rolls, 172
Tan Tan Ramen, 71
Tartar Sauce
    Crab Cakes, 183
    Crispy Fish Sandwiches with Tartar Sauce, 55
    Fish and Chips, 187
    Fried Calamari, 191
    recipe, 247

Teriyaki Chicken, 128
Teriyaki Sauce
    recipe, 249
    Wing Platter, 236
textured vegetable protein (TVP), 13
    Italian Meatballs, 34
    Meat Crumbles, 33
    Pad Kra Pao, 202
    Tan Tan Ramen, 71
Thai basil leaves
    Chicken Pho, 101
    Pad Kra Pao, 202
    Thai Chicken Red Curry, 98
Thai Chicken Red Curry, 98
Thai Sweet Chili Sauce
    Bang Bang Sauce, 246
    Crab Rangoon, 188
    recipe, 246
TikTok, 7
tofu, 13
    The Best Frozen Tofu Technique, 39
    Buffalo Burgers, 48
    Chicken 3.0, 24
    Chicken Nuggets, 152
    Chicken Parmesan, 155
    Deli Ham, 22
    Gochujang Chicken Sandwiches, 44
    Hot Dogs, 30
    Sausage, 31
    Sofritas, 140
    Tofu Bahn Mi, 220
Tofu Bahn Mi, 220
tomatoes, canned
    Birria Tacos, 90
    Butter Chicken, 144
    Chicken Parmesan, 155
    Chili, 106
    Gumbo, 102
    Italian Meatball Soup, 105
    Sausage and Peppers, 205
tomatoes, fresh
    Barbecue Chicken Wraps, 239
    BLT, 201
    Ceviche, 120
    Chipotle Chicken Tacos, 116
    Gumbo, 102
    Gyros, 175
    No-Fuss Black Bean Burgers, 215
    Pad Kee Mao, 67
tomato juice, in Ceviche, 120
tomato sauce, in Enchiladas, 123
tortilla chips
    Ceviche, 120
    Chicken Nachos, 115
    Chili, 106

tortillas
    Barbecue Chicken Wraps, 239
    Birria Tacos, 90
    Buffalo Chicken Snack Wraps, 51
    Carnitas Tacos, 85
    Chicken Fajitas, 86
    Chicken Quesadillas, 132
    Chicken Taquitos, 119
    Chimichangas, 136
    Chipotle Chicken Tacos, 116
    Enchiladas, 123
    Fish Tacos, 184
    Paneer Kathi Rolls, 223
    Roasted Veggie Quesadilla, 216
    Sofritas, 140

U

umami taste, ingredients for, 14

V

Velveeta, in Chicken Nachos, 115
vital wheat gluten
    Beef, 28–29
    Chicken 1.0, 20
    Chicken 2.0, 21
    Chicken 3.0, 24
    Deli Ham, 22
    Hot Dogs, 30
    Italian Meatballs, 34
    Meat Crumbles, 33
    Pad Kra Pao, 202
    Sausage, 31
    seitan made with, 13
    Steak with Garlic-Chive Butter and Asparagus, 168–169
    Tan Tan Ramen, 71

W

Wing Platter, 236
wonton wrappers
    Crab Rangoon, 188
    Spicy Wontons, 143

Y

yogurt, in Paneer Kathi Rolls, 223. *See also* Greek yogurt

acknowledgments

To my grandma, who encouraged me to cook from a young age and taught me my very first recipes. I'm sad to report they have yet to land me a husband, but I'm keeping the faith alive.

To my dad, who raised me as a single parent since I was six and who has always been my biggest cheerleader. Without your love, fierce protection, and countless sacrifices, I wouldn't be where I am today.

To Nigora, who has been a wonderful source of love and support over the years. You have taught me the virtue of patience, and you're the most naturally talented cook I know.

To all of my wonderful friends, who provide constant encouragement, support, and joy in my life. **Edna,** you are the closest thing I've ever had to a sibling. Thank you for including me in your family, making me feel loved, and constantly uplifting me. I wouldn't have survived law school or, like, most of life without you. **Victoria,** I have been able to rely on you consistently anytime I've needed warm words of encouragement and a judgment-free zone. You are a safe space, and I'm so grateful to have you in my life. **McKenna,** I know public declarations make you uneasy, but I never would have had the courage to quit my job and pursue writing this book if it wasn't for the conversation we had on our last night in Paris. You've always believed in me so purely and genuinely that it's made me want to believe more in myself. You've improved my life for the better in more ways than you could ever imagine. **Emily and Grace,** my little ladies. You were there every step of the way, from my first Instagram post to quitting my job. I will never take for granted the hours you've spent helping me choose the perfect photos or filters for my feed, organizing my blog posts, or listening to my incoherent rants on Marco Polo.

To Olivia, the best editor a girl could hope for. Thank you for your constant understanding, support, and reassurance. You've guided me off the ledge more times than I can count throughout this process, and I sleep well at night knowing I made the right decision by choosing you to work with on this book. I couldn't have dreamed of anyone better.

To my team at Aevitas, who believed in my vision for this book from the start. **Todd, Jack,** and **Lauren,** thank you for taking a chance on me.

To my food photography team, who brought this book to life. **Kelley, Ashley,** and **Lovoni,** thank you for all of your hard work, incredible creativity, and attention to detail. Your talents really made this book shine.

To Becky, for coming up with such kickass designs. You managed to peer into my brain and put my vision onto paper, and you are brilliant.

To DK, thank you for letting me live out a lifelong dream to write a cookbook. I am forever grateful.

about the author

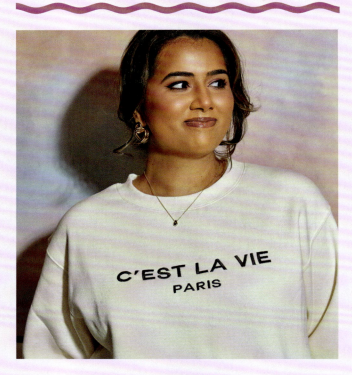

Shreya Walia is a lawyer turned social media personality who began her online cooking journey in 2020, at the start of the pandemic. A vegetarian for more than a decade, Shreya has discovered many tips, tricks, and techniques to create a vast variety of flavorful meatless dishes. She aspires to create a judgment-free zone for her audience to explore the richness and diversity of vegetarian cuisine, whether they are vegetarian, vegan, or simply plant-curious. She manages her online business, Shreya's Kitchen, from her home in the Pacific Northwest alongside her best friend and favorite companion, a goldendoodle named Charlie.